Formative Leadership

M000208478

This exciting new book is for school leaders who are interested in transforming their school and district practices. Discussing issues that impact students, teachers within their classrooms, and the larger school community, *Formative Assessment Leadership* explores how leaders can implement effective professional development and positive change in their schools. Breaking down formative assessment into manageable, understandable parts, the authors provide:

- An exploration of what formative data based decision making looks like
- Scaffolding that enables school leaders to effectively integrate processes into their own school structure
- Discussion of potential barriers to success and how to overcome these challenges
- Practical examples that help ground the formative assessment leadership concepts
- A range of worksheets and templates to help implement formative assessment leadership in your schools.

Karen L. Sanzo is Associate Professor and Program Coordinator of Educational Foundations and Leadership at Old Dominion University, Norfolk, Virginia.

Steve Myran is Associate Professor of Educational Foundations and Leadership at Old Dominion University, Norfolk, Virginia.

John Caggiano is Executive Director of Elementary School Leadership, Hampton City Schools, Hampton, Virginia.

Formative Assessment Leadership

Identify, Plan, Apply, Assess, Refine

Karen L. Sanzo, Steve Myran, and John Caggiano

Routledge
Taylor & Francis Group

NEW YORK AND LONDON

First published 2015
by Routledge
711 Third Avenue, New York, NY 10017

and by Routledge
2 Park Square, Milton Park, Abingdon, Oxon OX14 4RN

Routledge is an imprint of the Taylor & Francis Group, an informa business

© 2015 Taylor & Francis

The right of Karen L. Sanzo, Steve Myran, and John Caggiano to be identified as authors of this work has been asserted by them in accordance with Sections 77 and 78 of the Copyright, Designs and Patents Act 1988.

Library of Congress Cataloging-in-Publication Data
Sanzo, Karen.
Formative assessment leadership : identify, plan, apply, assess, refine / Karen L. Sanzo,
   Steve Myran, John Caggiano.
      pages cm
   Includes bibliographical references and index.
   1. Educational leadership.   2. School management and organization.   3. Educational tests and measurements.   4. Educational evaluation.   5. Educational change.   I. Myran, Steve.
II. Caggiano, John.   III. Title.
   LB2805.S266 2014
   371.2—dc23
   2014013323

ISBN: 978-0-415-74465-2 (hbk)
ISBN: 978-0-415-74466-9 (pbk)
ISBN: 978-1-315-76994-3 (ebk)

Typeset in Optima
by Apex CoVantage, LLC

Contents

Preface

Today schools are inundated with data, and the call to utilize this information to promote school improvement is more intense than ever. The pressure on both teachers and school leaders to effectively navigate this challenging territory can be daunting. One of the most important aspects of success in the growing data driven school context is the effective formative use of data, that is, using data in iterative ways to guide what happens next in the instructional process. However, just what this looks like within a school is complex and involves an interrelated set of skills and knowledge that can be challenging to master, particularly when educators are already stretched thin in terms of their time and energy. This book is designed as a guide to principals, assistant principals, department chairs, or anyone in an instructional leadership role, to help them work through the process of formative data based decision making.

Whereas much of what has been written about formative assessment is focused on the student and the classroom, we emphasize these principles and practices are also critical to school level data based decision making and instructional leadership. We take the position that the best evidence about what promotes learning points to three key issues: (a) learners must be active and deliberative agents in their own efforts, (b) the teachers' role is to facilitate the development of these increasingly independent learning behaviors, and (c) everyone else in the learning organization has the role of facilitating the previous two issues. The principles of formative assessment provide a powerful and empirically based set of tools that instructional leaders at any level can use to facilitate opportunities for students to be more deliberate and active learners. In the current accountability climate, in which there are so many pressures to teach to the test, formative assessment provides school leaders with a set of concepts and strategies to overcome these pressures and to help teachers elevate their instructional practices and for students to gain greater command over their own learning.

In this book we conceptualize schools as centers of inquiry where formative data based decision making functions as a means of involving educators directly in a discovery process about instruction and learning. This book utilizes an iterative cycle of inquiry, discovery, and action rooted in a purposeful set of strategies designed to directly demonstrate sound formative assessment practices. This discovery process provides the scaffolding for educators to articulate theory from their own practice and develop and fine tune practical skills. Perhaps Judith Warren Little (1981) said it best when she stated that "school improvement is most surely and thoroughly achieved when teachers engage in frequent, continuous, and increasingly concrete and precise talk about teaching practice" (p. 527). The cycle of formative data based decision making outlined in this book is designed to do just that.

We have structured this book to serve as a guide for district leaders, building-level administrators, and teacher leaders ready to embark on a thoughtful school-improvement journey. In the first two chapters we discuss principles of formative assessment, the role of leaders and the importance of integrating students into the process, among other concepts that support formative assessment leadership. We then turn to discussing the cycle of formative data based decision making, which we have developed and refined after a number of years of working with teachers and school leaders in urban, suburban, and rural schools. The cycle involves an Identify phase, during which teams of educators review the multiple measures of data to unearth patterns of student error, misconceptions, and student strengths along with related patterns of instructional weaknesses and assessing the conditions for fostering the development of the whole child. Given this foundational understanding of the factors that shape student learning, the Planning phase helps teachers plan instructional interventions that will directly address the challenges that were identified. Next, during the Apply phase teachers carry out their planning while gathering formative data along the way in order to assess its effectiveness. Last, during the Refine phase, educators review data and make assessments about the impact of their plans and make data informed adjustments in preparation for the next iteration of the cycle. This section is followed by a set of tools to support the cycle of formative data based decision making that includes several data scenarios and a host of worksheets and handouts to help facilitate the leadership of the cycle.

We believe school leaders who are prepared to thoughtfully use the cycle we have outlined in this book will be able to more fully harness the talents of the teachers in their schools and the capacity of the students to learn. The role of the school leader, as we have conceptualized it in this book, is to serve as a facilitator to this approach and support teachers in proactively developing and refining their skills and fostering students as deliberate and active agents in their own learning. The strategies outlined in this book will help build the needed organizational capacity within schools for sustained growth and improvement.

Explanation of How the Book Is Structured

We take an approach that is grounded in the concept of schools as centers of inquiry, as well as ideas about how involving educators directly in a discovery process invests them in both practical skills and knowledge and deeper conceptual underpinnings. An inquiry based approach provides a way practitioners can begin to blur the lines between theory and practice and be less skeptical about using evidence to support their daily practice. As such, this book is structured to enable school' leaders to walk teacher groups through a practical and purposeful set of strategies designed to directly demonstrate sound formative assessment practices.

The book is a guide for district leaders, building-level administrators, and teacher leaders ready to embark on a thoughtful school improvement journey. In the first two chapters of this book we discuss principles of formative assessment, the role of leaders, integrating students into the process, and other important background knowledge that support formative assessment leadership. We then turn to discussing the **Cycle of Formative Data Based Decision Making (DBDM).** We outline the five steps of this process and discussion associated with the steps of the cycle. The cycle was developed after a number of years working with various schools and school districts. This cycle is the blending of a number of experiences supported by the research in this area and involves five steps, as shown in Figure 1.

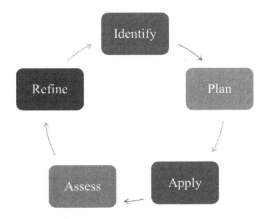

Figure 1 The Cycle of Formative Data Based Decision Making

We then provide tools to aid you in implementing this process. At the end of the book definitions of the key terms associated with formative DBDM are provided, as well as short case studies you can use with your leadership team as you calibrate your understanding of the implementation of the cycle. These examples provide firsthand experience with new or less familiar practices along with guiding questions that help educators articulate conceptual theory from their own experiences. **At the heart of this process is a set of strategies that will help your teachers integrate the students themselves into the process of learning.**

Laying the Groundwork for Formative Assessment

Introduction

This is a book for school leaders—principals, assistant principals, teacher leaders, school leadership team members, and others involved in guiding and leading schools to implement formative assessment practices in your school. In our research we have read many books and articles directed at engaging classroom teachers to make formative assessment an integral part of daily classroom practices. These are terrific resources and help cultivate—at the micro level—a classroom environment that embraces formative assessment. But we found something was missing "on the market" and "in the journals"—guidance for school leaders on how to start and guide the formative assessment process at the school level.

What does it mean to effectively use data to assist in making instructional decisions that will have a positive impact on student achievement? How do leaders do this? What types of data should be used? And by whom? And what process should be used? These are some of the questions we seek to answer for you in this book.

Halverson, Grigg, Prichett, and Thomas (2007) describe data based decision making (DBDM) as "link[ing] the results of summative testing to formative information systems that teachers can use to improve instruction across schools" (p. 163). That is a simple description for a complex educational concept. DBDM is not simple or procedural. According to Preuss (2007), DBDM must permeate school processes, emphasizing that DBDM "is a system of deeply rooted beliefs, actions, and processes that infuses organizational culture and regularly organizes and transforms data to wisdom for the purpose of making organizational decisions" (p. 10).

A Data Driven Culture

Today most educators find themselves working in very data driven school cultures. A number of federal and state requirements set on schools have caused school leaders, and the educational community as a whole, to critically examine our educational practices, as well as to delve into the unique characteristics of our student populations. Accountability efforts have forced educators to reexamine school structures, district practices, teacher evaluation, and assessment techniques. Although we have seen some truly remarkable gains in student achievement, clearly it is not enough as we still have many students who are failing to attain success in school and are leaving our educational environments unprepared.

Anyone who has spent a week in a school knows that teachers and school leaders are working hard to try to help their students be successful. Educators are inundated with strategies, processes, programs, and practices "specially designed" to increase student achievement. If you have been in the front office answering the phones or opening the mail, you also know that during any given week, numerous sales pitches selling prepackaged products designed to help our students meet and exceed "the standards" are given. But, as our national scores continue to demonstrate, there are students in our classrooms who are not being successful in spite of the myriad of items out there on the market and the newest trends surfacing.

Formative Assessment

In this book we are talking about what may be considered one of the newest trends in the accountability movement and the search for how to positively impact student achievement: formative assessment. **Formative assessment is actually *not new* and has a *very strong research base* to support its efficacy in helping students be successful.** Let us emphasize that formative assessment is a substantiated process that, when implemented correctly, contributes to academically successful learners. In fact, if you walk into one of your stellar teacher's classrooms—the type of teacher who teaches students who have been labeled as underperformers and who helps those students be overwhelmingly successful—you will see clear evidence of effective formative assessment practices.

Our goal in presenting this to you is to let you know that using formative assessment practices in your schools and classrooms is "not another thing to do" and "to add to the overflowing" plate of your staff members. **This is something good teachers do already.** We also want to peel away the misconceptions, the ambiguous processes of and barriers to formative assessment, and provide you the knowledge base and structure to begin a concerted effort within your school that has proved successful.

Formative assessment can be—and should be—embedded into the daily practices of your school. It fits well with school improvement and continuous learning processes, whether they may be professional learning communities, focus groups, response to intervention, or another structure. Smart teaching and smart formative assessment practices will help your students attain success.

It Is All About Productive Student Learning

Formative assessment goes to the heart of substantive student learning from kindergarten to high school and has critical links to virtually every aspect of quality instruction. But, through this book, we want to make sure that people really understand what formative assessment is all about. Right now formative assessment is a popular topic with a catchy phrase that is often thrown about in schools. There is a real danger that formative assessment can become "the trend of the moment," with all of the popular verbiage associated with it and absorbed into the dominant culture, becoming applied inconsistently without the fundamental understandings of why formative assessment is effective.

Self-Regulated *Learning Is Central to* Productive *Learning*

Formative assessment is a developmental process that involves cycles of goal setting, instruction, assessment, feedback, and adjustment both by learners and teachers. Formative assessment is the mechanism that makes it possible to effect those skills and behaviors in students. Formative assessment provides critical feedback to students while still working toward a learning goal. This makes formative assessment a fundamental part of pedagogy and critical to learning. Often, however, instructional practices are not successful in positively impacting student achievement because there is a lack of understanding revolving around self-regulated learning and formative assessment. There is an inescapable need for strong formative assessment leadership in our schools that emphasizes the power of engaging students in self-regulated learning.

Assessment Literacy

Because of our work in formative classroom assessment and DBDM in recent years, we have come to recognize the vital importance of assessment literacy for teachers and school leaders. In the current climate of high-stakes testing and accountability, assessment has taken on a narrow and often education- ally negative character. Unfortunately, preservice and in-service teacher and leadership training has not sufficiently addressed classroom assessment practices. This lack of training has led to a climate where teachers tend to use a "hodgepodge grade of attitude, effort, and achievement" (Brookhart, 1991, p. 36; Cross & Frary, 1996). It is also clear teachers use a variety of assess- ment techniques, even if established measurement principles are often vio- lated (Cross & Frary, 1996; Frary, Cross, & Weber, 1993; Gullickson, 1993; Plake & Impara, 1993; Stiggins & Conklin, 1992).

Although over the last two decades significant emphasis has been placed on using alternative assessments, such as performance assessments and portfolios (McMillan, Myran, & Workman, 2002), appropriate preser- vice and in-service training has not been adequate for teachers to effectively utilize these assessment practices. More important, current assessment prac- tices, and misunderstandings about them, are often counterproductive to deep and substantive learning.

Assessment literacy is critical to the effective use of data to make deci- sions; without both clear theoretical and practical understandings of assess- ment principles (both formative and summative) that become part of the regular structure of schools, programs will fail to capitalize on their poten- tial. **Moreover, it is the formative aspects of assessment that has the greatest impact on student learning.**

Formative Assessment Leadership Approach

Our unique approach focuses on the direct student-oriented nature of for- mative assessment and its necessity to breathe pedagogical life into other- wise lifeless efforts. **This approach is rooted in the substantial literature from across disciplines that highlight when students are provided with scaffolding that specifically prepares them to take active responsibility for their own learning they perform at significantly higher academic levels.** We refer to this as "active agency," or the students as active agents in their own learning (Skilton-Sylvester, 1999). This is similar to what Paul Pintrich (2003) called the intentional learner, which integrates a number of key learning behaviors that include motivation, self-regulation, and self-efficacy.

Active agency is central to formative assessment and in turn formative assessment is central to effective DBDM efforts. **Students must be active agents in their own learning.** Without a student having an active agent outlook, the formative assessment practices known to significantly improve student learning will not work.

Theory to Practice

Equally important is our distinctive way of conceptualizing and addressing the perennial concern over the theory-to-practice divide. Often there appears to be a disconnect between what is espoused in research circles and in higher education as educational theory and what actually happens in the schools and classrooms. We are interested in helping you make substantive student achievement gains and focus on where "the rubber meets the road"—what actually takes place in helping students learn. Throughout this book you will see we address bridging theory to practices through a framework that helps teachers and school leaders **articulate theory from their own contextualized professional experiences;** that is articulating theory *from* practice.

Most professional development (PD) programs do not create any lasting scaffolding for teachers to explore, try out, and refine their efforts. Too often PD activities last once or twice and have no framework for sustainability. The inability of most PD programs to allow this exploration means the various instructional and assessment strategies they were espousing do not bridge the gap between generalized theory and daily actual classroom practices. Without time and other critical resources, the transition from ideas to application in the classroom simply does not happen. Organizing teacher PD around such a model invites failure.

The Formative Assessment Professional Development Model

In our PD model, we address this challenge by advocating a framework that utilizes real-life, practical examples as building blocks to developing deep substantive understandings of formative assessment and DBDM principles.

It is crucial to use one's own contextualized professional experience. Our approach enables school leaders to help teachers understand how to effectively use sound formative assessment practices by capitalizing on educators' lived experiences working with students and by using this contextual knowledge to build "usable knowledge".

In our work promoting the use of formative classroom assessment strategies with teachers and school leaders in a variety of PD contexts, we have learned educators are not receptive to topically, academically abstracted, or thematic approaches to PD. Educators have been more receptive to incorporating aspects of formative assessment as part of their ongoing, day-to-day subject matter teaching responsibilities. Teachers want to know how the PD activity will have an impact on them immediately—they need to know the relevance. Without that, then the PD is useless.

Structure and Scaffolding

This book provides a structure for teams of teachers and school leaders to work together to develop deep contextualized understandings of effective formative assessment within the context of a DBDM atmosphere. More important, we provide the scaffolding for educators to articulate theory from their own practice and acquire purposeful and practical skills. We also address the many barriers to effective implementation of sound assessment practices assessment and DBDM models and make practical suggestions on overcoming these barriers.

We have found there is a large gap between what can be referred to as "Utopian" theories of how schools should operate and the day-to-day realities of school practice. Educators are often locked in the daily rigors of teaching and have a difficult time transitioning to new structures and practices, whereas academics look at the ideal without addressing in pragmatic terms how you bridge the vision and reality. The space between these two states is often left unexplored by PD processes, leaving no structure or support for educators and undermining the purposes of the intended PD provided and change process. Without any scaffolding to get you to that ultimate vision, you are undermining your own purposes for the effort. There is need to break down the theories without losing the deeper meaning and fidelity. We seek through this book to break down the formative DBDM process into an understandable and manageable process via a five-step cycle that assists leaders in implementing and leading the effort.

Using Data and Learning

Considerable research evidence points to how a formative approach to DBDM can foster significant improvements in teachers' uses of effective instructional practices and student achievement. "School improvement is most surely and thoroughly achieved when teachers engage in frequent, continuous, and increasingly concrete and precise talk about teaching practice" (Little, 1990, p. 527) what some have called "schools as centers of inquiry for adults as well as children" (Schmoker, 2004, p. 431). This inquiry-based approach to using data to improve instruction and student performance is built on a solid foundation of our field's best understanding about how students learn and how school organizations can work to better meet students' learning needs.

Although a detailed review of the learning sciences literature is outside the scope of this book, several key findings can be drawn which are straightforward and actionable. Learning requires:

1. engagement;
2. development of both factual knowledge and strong conceptual frameworks; and
3. self-monitoring of one's own efforts in progress towards a learning goal. (Bransford, Brown, & Cockring, 2000)

Instructional Core

It is certainly no mystery to educators that effective teaching is a key predictor of student success, nor that instructionally focused leadership is crucial to facilitate and support improvement in teacher quality. In fact, when principals and other leaders are well trained and focused on the instructional core they have a greater influence on student achievement (Robinson, 2007; Robinson, Lloyd, & Rowe, 2008). In the current high-stakes testing accountability environment, DBDM and assessment literacy are central aspects of the instructional core and require both teachers and school leaders to enhance their skills and knowledge of these areas.

Unfortunately, DBDM is often viewed as a panacea, a cure-all to the challenges schools face in this time of high pressure testing and accountability.

Although it does offer a well-organized set of strategies for bringing about improvements, much of the basis for the effectiveness of these strategies is not present in the instructional climate of many schools. In our work, we see frequent examples of educational organizations that, under tremendous pressure, use the rhetoric of data but that have little conceptual or practical understanding of what these processes are designed to accomplish. As such, they lack the organizational capacity to effectively use data to improve student learning.

Research in Educational Use

One of the reasons for the lack in the effective use of data to improve student learning is the considerable gap between research and practice and between the cumulative knowledge from the learning sciences and the daily work of educators working directly with students. The influence of research on practice, as Donovan, Bransford, and Pellegrino (1999) point out, is filtered through preservice and in-service education, textbooks and other training materials, public policy, and public opinion. Only a small number of educators are involved directly with design experiments and other firsthand generation of research evidence and as such are generally relegated to being the consumers of research. Because of the pervasive gaps between research and practice, often practitioners' firsthand experiences are in conflict with the research evidence. As a result, the culture of practice is often shaped less by evidence and more by historically resilient norms; practitioners may view research with skepticism and caution and as something that occurs outside of its domain.

The Leader's Role

What is needed then is an approach to utilizing formative DBDM designed to overcome the gaps between research and practice and allow educators to better capitalize on the potential of these practices. We take an instructional leadership approach in this book to support teachers in proactively developing and refining data based practices that support the core learning sciences principles of engagement, factual and conceptual knowledge, and self-monitoring learning by scaffolding opportunities for teachers to "engage in frequent, continuous, and increasingly concrete and precise talk about teaching practice" (Little, 1981, p. 12).

In this respect, the role of the school leader is to facilitate an environment that builds a center of inquiry around a broad spectrum of evidence and pushes to help the various stakeholders to narrow the gaps between research and practice. This view of the role of leadership is certainly not new or unique to formative DBDM, but it is consistent with the national standards of school leadership. National school leadership organizations highlight facilitating improvements, working with teachers and other stakeholders, focusing on learning and the importance of assessment and on school improvements, and building organizational capacity are all core skills and dispositions effective school leaders need.

In short, **the role of the school leader is to serve as a facilitator who assures the authentic involvement of teachers and other key stakeholders with an eye toward school improvement and toward building organizational capacity for improvements in student learning.** Although this book's purpose is narrowed toward the topic of formative DBDM, the approaches to leadership, working with teachers, and PD transcend this topic. Much can be learned about school improvement from the experiences of putting the cycle of formative DBDM into practice.

The Leader's Role in Facilitating Formative DBDM

The school leader's role in facilitating formative DBDM is critical because it provides a sound means of organizing school improvement efforts around evidence of how children learn and how school organizations build capacity. The processes outlined in this book allow educators to

- identify core instructional and achievement issues,
- set learning goals aligned with associated improvement efforts, and
- answer their own questions about the effectiveness of instructional practices and their impact on student achievement.

This deliberate process helps educators avoid rushing to implement new or less understood strategies, instead researching and refining interventions and making mid-course corrections and refinements based on their own evidence (Killion & Bellamy 2000). When teachers can see the effects of these approaches on their own students' learning behaviors and performance, they become more committed to, as well as more effective at, DBDM (Wade, 2001).

If schools are to become centers of inquiry where teachers engage in routine actionable discourse about practice, school leaders need to develop the skills to make sound data based decisions. With these skills, school leaders can foster an inquiry-minded school environment, where teachers learn to incorporate evidence in their daily practice and become more reflective, less reactive, and more open-minded in trying out solutions based in evidence they generated or gathered themselves (Wade, 2001).

Keeping Students at the Center

There is a position this book takes on the nature of learning that is fundamental to the fidelity of the strategies presented. This position is one that can be a notable challenge for our field because it requires a shift in perspective and some careful reflection and assessment of the organizational norms and habits of our schools as well as one's own individual assumptions and behaviors. The basis of this position is simple; all the best evidence about what promotes learning points to three key issues:

1. Learners must be active and deliberative agents in their own efforts.

2. The teacher's role is to facilitate the development of these increasingly independent learning behaviors.

3. Everyone else in the learning organization's role is to facilitate items 1 and 2.

The role of the instructional leader becomes central in creating and fostering the conditions for success. This is key to the purpose of this book because the formative use of data for sound instructional decision making is all about facilitating iterative growth.

This position is supported by powerful synthesis research (American Psychological Association, 1993, 1995; Hattie 2009; Marzano, 1998, 2001, 2003; Vosniadou, 2001). We have integrated tools reflecting this research into our cycle. This synthesis of research highlights that children need to be actively and socially involved in meaningful and applied learning activities, as well as engaged in novel and authentic problem solving that prompts curiosity and higher order thinking. Similarly, students should have learning experiences that promote understanding over memorization, create opportunities for them to transfer learning to new problems and learning goals, and engage them in deliberative practice. Experiences that promote the exploration of alternative explanations as well as the tentative nature of knowledge can help build depth and complexity of student understanding. Students should have opportunities to relate new information to prior knowledge and to restructure prior knowledge given new and deeper understandings as well as to explore the relationships between new learning goals and what they already know. Students should also have experiences where they see cognitive strategies modeled for them and are encouraged to develop metacognitive skills and greater self-awareness.

An important thread running through all of these findings is this requires the student to be actively and deliberatively engaged in learning. A docile student whose expectation is to passively receive content as it is delivered cannot experience the achievement benefits of the ideas summarized earlier. Similarly, teachers who see their roles as simply delivering standardized content and adhering to pacing guides and other prescriptive practices and who do not prompt the kinds of learning experiences outlined previously, cannot expect to see more than average to below-average gains in achievement in their classrooms. Among the most powerful strategies for fostering both greater student achievement and the refined teacher skill sets needed to facilitate these gains is formative feedback. As such, we have designed this book to help school leaders and teachers identify and collect data that can provide the types of feedback that can prompt teachers' deliberative engagement in their own professional growth as well as providing structure and opportunity for students to be active and deliberative agents in their own learning.

The majority of variance in learning can be accounted for by the students' own learning behaviors and by the instructional practices of the teacher; taken together it is the interactions between teachers and students where the action is and where much of the focus of this book takes place. More recent meta-analysis research suggests students' prior knowledge and learning behaviors account for approximately 50% of the variance in student learning and teacher characteristics and behaviors account for roughly 30% (Hattie, 2003, 2013). Others have ascribed larger percentages to student background and smaller percentages to teachers' impacts (Cornelius-White, 2007; Marzano, 2001; Meece, Herman, & McCombs, 2003; Weinberger &

McCombs, 2001). Although all the factors involved are complex and inter-related, and no simple or prescriptive solutions can be gleaned from this research, it is clear that how teachers select and design instructional strate-gies, communicate with students and assess progress, and in turn how stu-dents respond to these interactions has a large impact on student learning outcomes. The other factors such as principals, school climate, peer effects, and socioeconomic status are all indirect and account for much smaller percentages of the variance in student learning. What this tells us is that learning is most influenced by what students bring with them into the class-room, what the teacher does to support students' continued learning, and how the teacher/student relationship helps to mediate and improve these interactions.

Hattie (2013) asserted that the most powerful aspect of teaching is not so much in the planning and teaching of content, but in "what happens next"—how the teacher responds to students' interpretations, misunder-standings and applications of the content, how the teacher enables students to learn to use successful cognitive strategies such as summarizing, question-ing, clarifying and predicting, and, most important, how the teacher gives formative feedback that helps students focus on refining efforts and move closer to their proximal goals. In many respects, this "what happens next" aspect of teaching is what formative DBDM is all about: collecting infor-mation that helps educators respond to students' needs and facilitate their growing knowledge and self-efficacy.

With the preceding in mind, keeping students at the center of formative DBDM efforts is critical to the effectiveness of the process. Because about 80% (Hattie, 2003, 2013; Marzano, 2001) of the variance in student learn-ing can be accounted for by student factors and teacher factors, formative DBDM efforts that do not provide information, feedback, and support will have a smaller impact on student learning. Critical to this are the relationships formed between teachers and students. We know from Hattie's (2003, 2013) meta-analyses, these relationships are powerful predictors of student learn-ing with an average effect size of .72 (Hattie, 2013). This work emphasizes the highest effect sizes for different aspects of teacher–student relationships were non-directivity, empathy, warmth, and encouraging higher order think-ing. Although students' prior knowledge and background does play a signifi-cant role in learning, positive teacher–student relationships mediate learning in important ways. Cornelius-White (2007) found that, after controlling for aptitude and prior learning, about 20% of the variance beyond these two factors in student outcomes was due to teacher–student relationships. Many formative assessment strategies can serve as effective means of promoting and enhancing these types of positive teacher–student relationships and, by extension, can help keep students at the center of your efforts.

Inevitably, learners (all learners, including teachers and school administrators) experience frustration and failure. In fact, the Piagetian theory that we all learned in our teacher education programs reminds us this moment of disequilibrium (Piaget, 1968, 1971) is critical to learning. When students' current skills and knowledge (schema) do not adequately support new learning, they experience an imbalance between what they currently can do and what the new stimulus requires. For learners to regain this balance, or what Piaget called equilibration, they must develop new schema or adapt current skills and knowledge. This is the moment when learning takes place, when new or refined schema are developed that help learners restore balance. The uncomfortable moment when learning something new is frustrating is essential to learning and is our opportunity for growth, not failure.

2 | Understanding Assessment

What Is Formative Assessment, and Why Is It So Important?

What Is Formative Assessment?

The concept of formative assessment is not new or novel, having its roots in program assessment. Scriven (1967) first highlighted the differences between formative and summative assessment decades ago. This was followed in short order by Bloom (1968) incorporating formative assessment as a central component of *Learning for Mastery* and later writing the *Handbook of Formative and Summative Evaluation* (Bloom, Hastings, Madaus, & Baldwin, 1971). In 1986 Fuchs and Fuchs published a meta-analysis that investigated the effect of systematic formative evaluation with high-functioning special education populations and highlighted the positive impacts on student learning.

About 10 years later, Black and Wiliam (1998) published a more comprehensive meta-analysis and reported that typical effect sizes from the effective use of formative assessment practices were between .4 and .7. These effect sizes are larger than most other reported effects from various educational interventions and highlight the importance of formative assessment. **Although formative assessment is certainly not new, most school and school district assessment programs have yet to adopt a truly formative mind-set.** This may be in part because teachers often base their grading and assessment practices on their own educational philosophies and on what they see as best for their students (McMillan & Nash, 2000). Additionally, teacher and leadership training has not adequately addressed these skills in educators. Often, this leads educators to mistakenly use formative assessment practices through a summative lens, which actually undermines the potential of these effective practices.

A Process

Formative assessment provides a process for teachers and students to be engaged in a continuous cycle of assessment and feedback. This helps to clarify learning goals, as well as to assess progress toward those goals, enabling students and teachers to adjust learning and instruction resulting from assessment information. During the cycle of formative DBDM you and your team will develop school-level and classroom-level learning intentions, which are the primary areas of content and/or instructional focus. These learning intentions are critical for helping teachers and students develop and refine learning goals and with continuously self-assessing their progress compared to these clarified goals and learning intentions.

Formative assessment differs from summative assessment primarily in that it is a developmental way of evaluating the progress toward a specified goal. Summative assessment is simply the final evaluation of the degree to which the goal was met. Formative assessment provides a way to assess progress toward the goal and to identify areas that need to be adjusted to better meet the goal. Feedback is a critical aspect of formative assessment. As Gipps, McCallum, and Hargreaves (2000) pointed out, formative assessment takes place during the course of teaching and is used essentially to feed back into the teaching and learning process.

More specifically, students gain increased control over their own learning when they have opportunities to participate in clarifying their own **goals**. Clarifying and communicating learning intentions and involving students more directly in goal setting, self-assessment, and self-monitoring can have a powerful impact on student learning. There is strong evidence that students who are able to articulate what they are learning have significantly better learning outcomes than those who cannot. Marzano (2006) and Stiggins and Chappuis (Chappuis, 2005; Stiggins & Chappuis, 2005) utilized three simple questions that teachers can use to prompt this greater focus and use of learning intentions: *Where am I going? Where am I now?* and *How can I close the gap?* We have modified this structure for the formative DBDM cycle:

- **Goal setting** (Where am I going?)
- **Self-assessment** (How am I doing compared to my goal?)
- **Self-monitoring** (How am I progressing toward the goal?)

This involves student active reflection and self-assessment. Assessments that do not lead to students reflecting on their performance play little or no role in student learning. An example of this would be a student throwing away a quiz without reviewing it. These types of assessments can actually undermine learning. When a student receives a summative grade without any feedback, this simply confirms that student's low self-perceptions. For example, the student may think, "I got a D, and that confirms I can't do math." You must ensure your assessments during an instructional unit lead students to assess their own performance in a productive way. This is a key point in formative assessment and can be very difficult at first because many students have learned to be passive recipients of information (a "sit and get" mentality)—you need to help them develop active orientations to learning.

Four Factors to Improve Learning

Learning is improved by effective Formative Assessment and depends on four simple factors:

1. **Forward feedback**
2. **Active involvement of students in their own learning**
3. **Adjusting teaching to take account of the results of formative assessment**
4. **A recognition of the profound influence assessment has on the engagement and self-efficacy**

A central concept of formative assessment is the need for students to be able to assess themselves and understand how to improve. In the classroom this means sharing learning goals with students, involving students in self-assessment, and providing feedback which leads to students understanding where they are and what steps to take next to reach the goal. **The most powerful moderator that enhances achievement is feedback.** As Hattie (1999) asserted, the most effective way of improving student learning is "dollops of feedback," that is, providing information about what a student does and does not understand and about what direction the student must take to improve.

Self-Assessment

The most fundamental form of assessment is self-assessment. That is, all quality assessment ultimately becomes a form of self-assessment. If not, then it is simply disregarded. In terms of learning and changing behavior, self-assessment is fundamental. The distinction between evaluative feedback and forward feedback helps illustrate this. Evaluative feedback, such as a letter grade or an "attaboy," does not provide any direction for the learner and can actually undermine future efforts. Forward feedback, on the other hand, provides information that students can use to adjust their performance as they work toward a learning goal. You need to view all assessment design from this standpoint, asking will the teacher and/or the student receive the assessment feedback in some form or another to self-assess, to set refined goals, and to seek information on how to move forward? If not, then you need to ask about the usefulness of the assessment design.

Assessment designs that do not meet these criteria can undermine learning by fostering dependence, because students look to teachers for judgments about learning standards and assurances that they are meeting the learning objectives. This dependence removes students from being responsible for assessing their own progress and for judging quality against some known objective and deprives students of the opportunities to develop the habits of lifelong learners.

Why Does Formative Assessment Matter?

Fullan (2001) has argued that eliminating the achievement gap will require the mobilization of the teacher workforce around assessment literacy. Similarly, Heritage, Lee, Chen, and LaTorre (2005) suggested "considerable investment in human capital will be required to develop assessment literacy and data analysis skills that will, ideally, reach from district to classroom level" (p. 38). Today, literacy means successfully transitioning from a primary focus on *assessment of learning* to a **balanced literacy of assessment of learning *and* for learning.**

As Black and Wiliam (1998) have discussed, solid evidence has shown formative assessment can raise standards of achievement. In the climate of high-stakes testing and accountability, assessment has become a key driver in school reform efforts. As our ideas about assessment have grown and adapted to the challenges of meeting the increasing demands of the No Child Left Behind (NCLB) legislation and of individual state standards, educators have advanced their assessment practices from a primarily summative use to the use of both summative and formative measures. But, as Stiggins (2006) has pointed out, in the current climate, formative assessment has sometimes taken on a narrow meaning. He asserts educators are now interpreting formative assessment to mean more frequently administered summative assessments to determine which students have not yet met state standards—what Stiggins described as an "early warning system." Opportunities for students and teachers to use assessment to make adjustments while still learning are rare in the climate of standards of learning, pacing guides, 9-week benchmark testing, and other pressures prominent in the precision test preparation climate schools now operate.

Although the NCLB legislation has its share of detractors, it has been critical in publicly spotlighting historic performance gaps between various student subgroups, has made a greater commitment to raising all students' achievements to a set minimum standards, and holds schools accountable for meeting these benchmarks. One of the unfulfilled promises of the standards and accountability movement, however, is the shifting from sorting students, based on achievement, to helping all students meet a set of comprehensive standards. Well implemented formative assessment strategies are one powerful tool for helping to meet this promise.

A Fundamental Shift

In our view, in order to meet this promise, a fundamental shift that transitions educators from seeing student achievement as largely the product of innate capacity, family background, and parental support (Thrupp, Mansell, Hawksworth, & Harold, 2003) to being greatly influenced by what happens in the roughly 6.5 hours students spend in school each day must take place.

Because assessment is the primary means by which accountability is measured, it has come to dominate much of the educational landscape. In the past, assessment was used primarily to assess a student's place within the continuum of academic achievement. These assessments have been primarily summative in nature and have rarely been used to identify the deeper school environment, teacher quality, and pedagogical and cognitive issues that can undermine student learning. Instead, student assessment merely confirmed a student's place in the socioeconomic order and failed to be used diagnostically to identify both instructional and learning concerns that could be used to refine and strengthen the learning environment.

In part because of this lack of formative evaluation of assessment data, few students have escaped their particular position within this continuum, greatly limiting their social and economic mobility. Although contemporary educational practices, including assessment and accountability, have attempted to overcome these historic barriers, schools and the larger field of education are resistant to change, and the shift from a largely summative orientation about assessment to a formative one that recognizes the student as innately capable is a greater challenge than merely instituting policy and implementing new practices.

Assessment as a Powerful Tool

Today, due to significant investments, research, and implementation efforts of formative assessment practices, assessment can be a powerful tool for helping all students achieve. Research in the past number of years in formative assessment is well established and shows its profound impact on student achievement (Black & Wiliams; 1998; Hattie & Marsh, 1996; Hattie & Timperley, 2007; Stiggins, 2007, Thompson & Wiliam, 2007).

Benchmark testing, data driven decision making, and other formative uses of assessment data have gained wide support as means of improving student learning. Although summative assessments are critical to accountability, they are not particularly effective in supporting teaching and learning. **Formative assessments, particularly those used directly in the classroom with students, hold the greatest promise for improving students' substantive learning.** Yet these powerful teaching and learning tools have been very slow to be picked up by schools and strategically incorporated into their school improvement plans, or to be incorporated into university preservice teacher training and university leadership preparation programs, as well as in-service teacher and administration professional development.

Meeting the Standards

For many school leaders, meeting the standards is often attempted through the alignment of the standards to the curriculum and is further specified through pacing guides. In addition, frequent testing has become more commonplace with quarterly and even semiweekly testing has becoming increasingly common. As Starratt (2004) pointed out, many schools and districts have resorted to more frequent testing, which has contributed to inauthentic learning. Similarly, Mintrop and Trujillo (2005) stressed the increasing pressure on teachers to continually raise student test scores has created a situation in which principals have become "conduits of pressure." This has created an accountability environment where pacing guides, the alignment of standards with the curriculum, and an increasing frequency of testing have overshadowed our significant shared understanding of quality instruction.

Simple alignment of standards to curriculum with frequent monitoring through testing, however, is a house of cards devoid of instructional classroom assessment practices known to improve student learning. **Clearly, deep, substantive learning involves much more than surface alignment.** Test scores, on their own, hold little promise of promoting students' ability to produce and use knowledge. In order to foster this flexible and responsive learning, school leaders and teachers need "assessment literacy" (Earl & Fullan, 2003).

Climate of High-Stakes Testing

In the current climate of high-stakes testing and accountability, assessment has taken on a narrow and often educationally negative character. Unfortunately, preservice and in-service teacher and leadership training has not sufficiently addressed instructionally beneficial assessment practices. This lack of education and of training has led to a climate in which teachers tend to use a "hodgepodge" of grading and assessment strategies (Brookhart, 1991, p. 36; Cross & Frary, 1996) and educational leaders have remained "unschooled in the principles of sound assessment" (Stiggins, 2002, p. 45) and have expressed feelings of powerlessness and lack of confidence in this area (Earl & Fullan, 2003). Furthermore, few states require appropriate competence in assessment as a condition to be licensed as a principal (Stiggins, 2002). This is unfortunate given that assessment literacy is a powerful tool for school improvement (Fullan, 2001; Spillane, Halverson, & Diamond, 2001).

Because of this lack of assessment literacy, teachers use a variety of assessment techniques, even if established measurement principles are often violated (Cross & Frary, 1996; Frary et al., 1993; Gullickson, 1993; Plake & Impara, 1993; Stiggins & Conklin, 1992). Although over the last two decades significant emphasis has been placed on using alternative assessments, such as performance assessments and portfolios (McMillan et al., 2002), appropriate preservice and in-service training has not been adequate for teachers to effectively utilize and for leaders to effectively facilitate these assessment practices. More important, current assessment practices and misunderstandings about assessment are often counterproductive to deep and substantive learning.

You Become What You Measure

An imbalanced notion of assessment, with a primary, or even exclusive, focus on the assessment of learning is a significant danger to school improvement and student learning. Working harder within the confines of the current thinking about assessment quickly bumps into the functional limitations of a narrow or imbalanced notion of assessment. As Wergin (2003) asserted, *you become what you measure,* and this could not be truer than in the case of standards-based assessments.

Chasing the measure, or what has been deferred to as "goal displacement" (Blau & Scott, 1962), runs the risk of underestimating the need to teach the higher order cognitive skills widely recognized as being necessary for advancement to upper level courses and as a fundamental life skill in today's complex society. A primary focus on teaching to the test can take the life out of school programs and deflect teaching from its real purposes and from the real intent of your state's identified learning standards and the requisite competencies for subjects.

Measuring Via Formative Assessment

A formative assessment approach using testing has the potential to provide teachers with diagnostic data that, with today's technology, can be descriptive to the individual substandard and individual learner basis. This information generated by district-wide assessments of reasonable quality on a 9-week basis (Marzano, 2003) can provide a fair benchmark from which to work.

The formative assessment process using district-wide assessments, however, forges a double-edged sword typically inherent to statistics. The same application that produces formative data at a classroom or campus level can produce reports indistinguishable from those used by summative programs on a district level. Based on insights gleaned from these district and campus data, in a formative climate, one might expect a reallocation of resources to schools in need rather than actions more akin to classic uses of summative scores.

The summative use of data, however, establishes status scores and trends that can be used to generate milestones and expectations that translate into pressure on schools, principals, and teachers. This kind of pressure lends itself to inappropriate uses of results including use as a teacher evaluation tool, a principal evaluation tool, and is often the motivation behind teachers teaching to the test (Haertel & Herman, 2005), reallocating instructional time to unrelenting test preparation, drill and kill, and use of items cloned and re-cloned from released state exams (Popham, 2006) or district assessments.

The pressure created in some schools can lead to daily testing, gross reallocation of instructional time to those content areas considered more critical, such as reading and mathematics (Hannaway & Hamilton, 2008; Welsh, Eastwood, & D'Agostino, 2014) and reallocation of instructional time to test preparation. As noted by Spillane (2000), the consequences can also lead to sufficient pressure for teachers to leave the school, district, and—in the worst case—education altogether. This type of leadership impact on teacher efficacy has long been recognized (Tschannen-Moran, Woolfolk Hoy, & Hoy, 1998). This accountability pressure can manifest in other unintended and adverse ways. For example, the inappropriate use of pacing guides by teachers. Some teachers, for example, may finish their 9 weeks' pacing guide early but may not move on or provide enrichment activities. Instead, this has the unintended consequence of becoming a time for more drill and practice in order to have students score better on benchmark assessments, even though students have demonstrated their understanding of the topic.

A Formative Orientation About Learning, Instruction, and Classroom Management

The potential of formative classroom assessment has been well documented, but this view of the classroom changes the nature of the relationship between the teacher and the student. Teachers are no longer seen as the omniscient knowledge authorities and students as the passive recipient of that knowledge. Instead, **students take active responsibility for their own intellectual development and teachers facilitate this through assessment and instructional strategies** that involve students in what Skilton-Sylvester (2003) called "holistic task responsibility."

We have found this is a difficult transformation for stakeholders. Much of the effort asks the participants (teachers, school leaders, and university faculty/staff) to think and act differently from which we are generally acculturated. The assumptions about learning inherent in formative classroom assessment require a notably different orientation about the nature of knowledge and learning. This also requires iterative opportunities for teachers and educational leaders to utilize formative assessment strategies in their classrooms and in data team meetings to assess their effectiveness. This allows us to refine and develop these new skills over time.

Learning to Think Formatively

Although learning to think formatively is a challenge for all stakeholders, the rewards for doing so are great, and the logic to support this transformation, compelling. **Research in formative assessment and feedback highlight the greatest learning gains are achieved through strategies involving students directly and actively.** Strategies that leave the student as the passive recipient of instruction are less effective and in some cases can undermine learning.

According to Stiggins (2005a,b), formative assessment informs instructional decision making by providing information about how and what students are learning. More important, formative assessment encourages students to take responsibility for their own learning by engaging in self-assessment, reflection, goal setting, and monitoring and communicating their own progress. For students to engage in these proactive learning behaviors, teachers and leaders must update and refine current assessment practices in order to better support the development of these deep and substantive learning behaviors.

As Erickson (2007) pointed out, formative assessment is a fundamental part of pedagogy, and as such, it has critical links to virtually every aspect of quality instruction. Formative assessment strategies provide scaffolding for students to identify proximal goals, identify the characteristics of quality work, self-assess their progress, and adjust their performance to better meet the learning goal. These assessment behaviors are a key aspect of effective learning behaviors.

In support of this idea, Marzano's 1998 meta-analysis of research on instruction identified nine core instructional strategies that improve student learning. Of those nine strategies, setting goals and providing feedback and reinforcing effort and providing recognition, in particular, have important and direct links to formative assessment, whereas generating and testing hypotheses, activating prior knowledge, identifying similarities and differences, summarizing and note taking, and cooperative learning all have important links to formative assessment. Similarly, Hattie's (2013) meta-analyses highlighted that feedback is a particularly powerful instructional strategy. Feedback has its roots in formative assessment, and its fidelity is dependent on assuring it is used within a formative mind-set about assessment and instruction.

Effective Instruction and Classroom Management

As virtually every practicing teacher knows, effective instruction is dependent on effective classroom management. Many view this as the precursor to instruction; learning cannot occur in disruptive classrooms. Quality teacher-student relationships have been shown to predict 30 percent fewer discipline problems (Cornelius-White, 2007). This is not an issue of a teacher's personality but of specific behaviors that support sound relationships.

These behaviors are showing appropriate levels of authority and cooperation and an awareness of high-needs students (Marzano, 2003). Additionally, teachers need to provide a balance between demonstrating consequences for unacceptable behavior and the benefits and rewards for good behavior (Stage & Quiroz, 1997). An important aspect of providing guidance and support for appropriate student behavior is establishing and understanding clear learning goals and success criteria, which means the teacher guides the student and provides substantive feedback about the student's progress toward learning goals, which have important links to formative assessment and highlight the centrality of this topic to effective teaching.

Formative Assessment in the Context of Data Driven Decision Making

As the era of accountability appears to be with us for the foreseeable future, many have paused to ask if our use of summative data provides decision makers with what they need to create learning cultures that enable students to achieve at advanced levels. The call for assessment literacy has been made, yet achieving goals beyond state accountability standards; that is, substantive learning and the habits of lifelong learning as well as eliminating performance gaps, remain elusive in many schools.

We argue the natural extension to the considerable investment in assessment and testing infrastructures to support accountability initiatives is DBDM within a formative assessment framework. Formative assessment scaffolds and supports student learning that goes beyond the basics of literacy and numeracy; supporting deep, substantive learning; closing achievement gaps; and show particularly effective results for low-achieving students. We believe our approach to DBDM within a formative assessment context can help advance the purpose of accountability well beyond simply meeting benchmarks.

Data Based Decision Making

Discussing formative assessment outside the context of DBDM is simply not possible. DBDM, also called evidence-based decision making and data driven decision making, among other names, is considered an integral component in our schools to help effect high student achievement. But, just as there are multiple ways to call the use of data to make sound and informed decisions to help impact student learning in schools, there are numerous definitions and opinions as to what DBDM truly is. Added to this is the fact that formative assessment is inextricably linked to sound decision making practices involving data. Therefore, we feel it is imperative to provide an overview of DBDM and of how formative assessment is embedded into this process.

What Is DBDM?

DBDM is the process of gathering, analyzing, applying, and sharing data to promote school improvement. Our experiences with schools have shown they have largely not viewed DBDM in a formative assessment context, but rather in a summative assessment context with a narrow view as to what qualifies as data. There needs to be an understanding of the key forms of data we should be using in our schools. Because of the standards-based environment and accountability testing, the bulk of decision making in data teams tends to be around quarterly assessments or using summative assessment results for remediation efforts. An important consideration must be recognized that although those benchmark data can be used formatively, this is not how they are principally designed.

The Multiple Measures of Data

As noted earlier, teachers and data teams often focus on summative forms of assessments designed to predict and report out end of quarter or school year student achievement. Typically these assessments are not designed with formative assessment purposes in mind. It is the formative feedback—feedback about the instructor, feedback about instruction, and feedback to the student about learning—through which learning takes place.

Teachers and teams should be focusing their attention on the types of data and DBDM that capitalizes on effective feedback. Too often, teachers and teams focus on data that look at differentiating students into subgroups by performance for remediation and enrichment rather developing deficient learning skills and knowledge areas. One contributor to this too-narrow scope of data analysis by educators is the lack of awareness of the multiple types of data that should be used in the decision making process.

In this section we present an overview of the Multiple Measures of Data (Bernhardt, 2003, 2013). References are provided in the back of this book on further resources to fully explore the multiple measures. The Multiple Measures of Data provides educators a vehicle to articulate the many types of data you are inundated with in your formative DBDM processes. We say inundated because there appears to be now so much data to analyze that it is often overwhelming. In fact, you will find this as one of the barriers to effective formative assessment practices later in this chapter. Schools that have not set in place a structure to categorize and articulate data will simply drown in data and will not use them effectively.

Also, without having definitive categories to identify types of data needed to use in the decision making process, some valuable pieces may be overlooked. Later on, you will find a discussion about terminological misconceptions that deter sound formative assessment and DBDM practices. Without having distinct, defined categories of data, you will find that your conversations with school staff are not being fully understood.

You each bring to the table your own mental models of what something should be. So, for example, you may think when you are discussing formative assessment with staff they understand the student is an *active agent* in their own learning. But, without having a common, accepted, and internalized definition of formative assessment and active agency, some teachers may think they are simply being asked to quiz and test their students on a more frequent basis and add more grades to their records for student summative evaluations. There is a clear gap between these two mental models that can be overcome by laying the foundational groundwork to a common understanding of concepts.

Multiple Measures and Continuous Improvement

School leaders can use the Multiple Measures of Data as a foundational component in their continuous school improvement process. In fact, having these four categories that incorporate both quantitative and qualitative data helps us to articulate the types of data teachers will use in their formative assessment practices. Bernhardt shares the types of data as demographics, student learning, perceptions, and school processes.

> *Demographics: Demographics help you understand your school's context. These types of data include race, language background, community information, school characteristics, and student data (gender, age, etc.). Demographics inform you about the context within which your school operates.*
>
> *Student Learning: Student learning data provide an understanding of how the instructional processes impact achievement. These types of data can include summative assessments, benchmark assessments, and standardized and norm-referenced tests, as well as formative assessments. Student learning data are an integral component in formative assessment; however, relying only on student learning data to inform instruction will not result in success for all students.*
>
> *Perceptions: Perceptual data, including information about values, beliefs, and perceptions of the community of learners, can significantly impact how students learn and staff members facilitate instruction (note we do not say "how teachers teach").*
>
> *School Processes: School process data include instructional strategies, schedules, school learning plan goals and objectives, and classroom practices and routines. Data collected can include types of programs being implemented in the school, instructional strategies, schedules, school improvement goals and action steps, and general classroom practices.*

We readily acknowledge the need for leaders to fully explore summative data, especially in this context of high-stakes accountability. But improvements in learning on the part of the student and in professional knowledge on the part of the educators come in the iterative, formative process. As such, the focus of formative assessment efforts should be largely centered on those forms of data known to improve performance. It is necessary to critically examine our uses of data and ask, "How can we transition typically summative associated data into more formative applications?" Leaders need to recognize that the NCLB data are designed for accountability purposes and often speak to expectations regarding minimum competencies. But summative data in some cases can and should be used formatively.

Forms of Data to Improve Performance

There is much merit in exploring school-based formative assessment processes to ensure these are being used at deep, substantive levels with the students actively involved. Because improvements in professional knowledge of the teacher and in learning by the student come in the iterative formative process, a data team's focus should be largely centered on those forms of data known to improve performance. For example, leaders can guide their staff to look closely at informal student observations and to use them in a formative manner. We tend to use those informal observations to confirm what we see in the accountability data. We do not always look at the informal assessments and ask from an instructional standpoint, "What is the teaching problem?"

With the preceding in mind, DBDM programs established within a formative assessment framework are not only a more effective means of capitalizing on assessment data; they also provide important support for quality instruction and classroom management. This is not to say that a formative assessment framework is a cure-all, but it does represent a number of central elements of quality teaching.

Given the importance of teacher quality as a predictor of student achievement (Marzano, 2003), capitalizing on the important links between teacher quality and formative assessment would be strategically prudent. Although formative assessment is an important topic in contemporary education and is gaining increasing exposure and credibility, it, nonetheless, represents a different orientation about the nature of assessment, as well as the nature of the role of the teacher and of the student. Because of this, leaders must consider pragmatic steps to help educators negotiate the various hurdles that a paradigm shift of this nature involves.

Integrating Your Staff's Approach to DBDM

In our own work, we have not found educators to be receptive to a topically or academically abstract or thematic approach to professional development. Instead, we have found that they have been more receptive to incorporating aspects of formative assessment as part of their ongoing, day-to-day responsibilities. As a result, we have developed a purposeful approach to working with educators that views the implementation of new efforts as requiring both a pragmatic and a developmental approach.

We provide a framework for an iterative approach that addresses educators' need to develop background knowledge of the requisite practices and the ability to work collaboratively to plan, try out, evaluate, and share their experiences with other educators tied to the needs and priorities of the schools and their day-to-day needs in the classroom. This model represents a professional development approach and school reform model that better utilizes the strengths of school personnel and links progress and developing teacher quality to student performance.

In short, our model

- facilitates strategically incorporating the specific needs of the schools around the initiative,

- encourages and provides a structure for educators' active collaboration with colleagues and provides outside support and information they can use to substantially enhance their professional expertise,

- provides a means of directly linking teacher professional development with improved student academic achievement, and

- offers a potential alternative to the often ineffective or minimally effective approach to supporting professional development in public schools. (Borko, 2004)

Why Practical Examples Are Important

As Fullan (2007) suggested, the majority of educational innovations have failed to endure because they have assimilated innovations into existing beliefs and perceptions. This is what Vander Ark (2002) has described as mere overlays on existing school climates. Addressing these beliefs and perceptions as part of improvement efforts is important to bringing about lasting change. However, addressing these perceptions alone does little to promote the kind of improvement you seek. As such, our approach is designed to help overcome these perceptual barriers by providing practical guidance and purposeful activities that exemplify the fundamental principles of formative assessment and that promote normative changes that help to avoid the concerns of assimilation and overlay.

Our work with teachers and school leaders has led us to develop an approach to professional development that seeks to overcome many of the pitfalls inherent in the standard approach. Our model seeks to develop a culture of collaborative inquiry in which the teachers and educational leaders work side by side in their own school context and links new and transformed practices to student performance.

Our work has taken us into numerous classrooms across multiple school districts and provided us with significant opportunities to make detailed observations about the contemporary challenges in public schools. Based on teacher and administrator feedback, observations, and ongoing dialogue, we determined that our professional development activities needed, above all else, to address educators' daily pragmatic needs in order to have any hope of becoming a normative part of school life. Although we identified a number of important factors to successful implementation of formative assessment practices, we have found that **providing educators with practical strategies they could readily use in their classrooms and with their data teams was paramount to successful implementation of these new approaches to data and assessment.**

Without the opportunity to see firsthand how various strategies work and opportunities to discuss experiences using them, teachers and administrators lose interest and the process loses credibility. These practical examples serve a number of important functions. First, they provide a relatively quick firsthand experience with a particular strategy, and second, help to exemplify for the teacher and administrator a key concept or theory. We avoid the challenges implicit in a theory to practice approach by starting with a carefully selected research based strategy and engineering opportunities to experience firsthand the underlying concept or theory, thereby articulating theory from practice. Articulating theory from practice is much more in alignment with the realities of educators' work lives and professional development needs.

Our experience and research suggests educators' willingness and commitment to utilizing formative assessment strategies may be mediated by their summative/formative orientations toward classroom assessment. That is, teachers' understanding of assessment as something that involves the student as active agents in their own learning may foster more effective uses of formative assessment strategies.

Providing Teachers With Experiences

Our experiences have taught us practicing educators need opportunities to articulate theory from practice, thereby using their pragmatic daily experience to express a deepening professional outlook on their work. Educators need opportunities to "see" the practical manifestations of theory translated into their own experiences. Without these examples, as well as ongoing follow-up, there is little hope of educators effectively utilizing or sustaining this learning.

As we have gained experiences in teaching graduate courses and providing professional development services to teachers and school leaders, along with our experiences as teachers and school administrators, we have grown to appreciate the importance of learning experiences that balance theory with applied skills and knowledge. Maintaining this balance is a challenge.

If there is a very heavy focus on theory, staff may feel frustrated that they are not developing the practical skills and knowledge they can readily put to use in their work. On the other hand, if too much attention is paid to applied knowledge, staff will not develop a foundation of theory and professional knowledge that is important to high-fidelity implementation of formative assessment practices.

Assuring Balance

This theory-to-practice gap is commonplace in the field of education and highlights the need for instructional approaches that scaffold learning experiences in order to maintain a theory/practice balance. To assure this balance, our approach to PD around formative assessment involves four key areas:

1. Identifying practical examples that exemplify key concepts that students can draw from to develop deeper and more generalizable professional skill and knowledge

2. Providing contextual opportunities to test and refine evolving knowledge in the field or in some relevant context

3. Creating formative feedback opportunities to provide real-time information to staff about their performance that allow them to adjust and strengthen their professional growth

4. Providing opportunities for peer interaction so that individuals can share their expertise and experience with each other to enhance knowledge development and professional networking

We point out that in absence of these practical examples and ongoing interactions to address professional learning questions, professional development efforts have little hope of being effectively utilized or sustained. As you engage in your own process of formative DBDM, it is incumbent on you and your leadership team to identify contextually relevant examples that you can use as you introduce and work through the process. Without these practical examples, used from your own school's and your district's experiences, it will be difficult for teachers to see the direct relevancy and application to their own practice. Abstract examples presented in more theoretical ways will not garner the type of understanding and impact you are looking for as opposed to real-world examples from your own work.

Understanding Barriers to Successful Implementation

Before you begin to implement a new structure into your school learning paradigm, it is critical to understand your organizational structure, the current status of assessment practices in your school, and the overall conceptual understanding of you and your teachers of formative assessment. We have all learned that it is impossible to jump into a new situation, and be successful, without understanding the organization. Change takes time and should be deliberate and well planned. If your school is new to the concept of deep integration of formative assessment practices in the instructional setting, then you should be prepared to engage in this process from a "second-order change" mind-set.

The research literature, as well as our own experiences as school leaders, informs us that there are a number of factors to be aware of when engaging in a change process. Although we do not engage in an in-depth exploration of the myriad factors to be aware of from a change perspective, we do think it is important to be aware of potential barriers when leading a process to integrate deep formative assessment practices into your school. There are a number of barriers to the effective implementation of a DBDM process. Understanding these barriers in relation to your school will help alleviate potential concerns later on in the process.

It is important to understand the broader context—the district and your external school community—but for our purpose in this book we are focusing internally on the school. It is, therefore, crucial to conduct a needs assessment related to DBDM and formative assessment prior to the start of this process. In saying that, we want to emphasize this is not a step in the process that only needs to occur once. You must conduct periodic needs assessment activities—essentially using the formative assessment process highlighted in this book for your activities within the school.

Potential Barriers to the Process

If "knowing is half the battle," then recognizing potential barriers that may hinder your formative assessment process are important to your success and overcoming potential obstacles. Barriers identified in the literature include a lack of common understanding of key terms, numerous and confusing models, fear of data being used in a punitive manner, and fear of what data might reveal. Many educators have the desire to use data to make informed decisions, but "few educators have the preparatory background to engage in such analysis and reflection" (Wayman, Midgley, & Stringfield, 2006, p. 189). Teachers have training as content specialists rather than in how to use data to make instructional decisions.

Wayman, Cho, and Johnston (2007), in their evaluation of data use in the Natrona County School District, found teachers claimed to use data, but "they were consistently vague about actions taken from using these data" (p. 24). We suggest examining the preparation backgrounds of your teaching staff to better understand their level of assessment awareness from an instructional perspective. In fact, we advocate for including questions about formative assessment practices in interviews of new teachers to the school. In the following, we have provided examples of interview probes and questions, but we advise you to contextualize your questions for your unique school setting.

Potential Data Focused Interview Questions

- Describe several strategies that can be used to check for student understanding at the end of a lesson.
- Discuss why it is important for a teacher to be able to effectively assess students' understanding of a lesson's learning intentions/objectives.
- From the standpoint of alignment (written, taught, and tested curriculum), please share the importance of designing formative assessments that address both the content and cognitive level of a given standard.

- What are several strategies that can be used to assess student learning during the lesson and at the conclusion of instruction?

- How do you go about determining whether lesson objectives were met?

- How do you plan to provide feedback to the students?

- How will the students be assessed by both the teacher and by the students themselves?

- Where do you build in time for student reflection and self-assessment in your lessons?

- What measures will you have in place to seek feedback from all of your students to ascertain whether they have understood and are able to demonstrate understanding of the lesson objectives?

- How will you use formative assessment results to drive lesson planning?

- How will you assess your students throughout the lesson and at closure to ensure that the lesson objectives have been met?

- How will you ensure that students understand how they are doing and support students' self-assessment?

- Describe how you go about identifying students in need of intervention for a given skill. How do you monitor student progress in your classroom on an ongoing basis?

Formative Assessment Leadership emphasis is at the classroom level. Teachers are directly where the action takes place in schools, and therefore, they must be able to effectively make sound instructional decisions based on data using a solid process. Unfortunately, teachers have not always been considered an integral part of the data use process (Wayman et al., 2006) and may or may not have the necessary training to understand and use data. Bernhardt (2004) has lamented the lack of professional development for teachers to understand why data are important and how data can make a difference in their teaching. Although we can espouse the need to disaggregate data to explore subgroups, identify achieve gaps, and point out in general areas where the curricula may be strengthened to improve student achievement, there has not been as much of an emphasis on how teachers themselves can utilize data to make good instructional changes in their daily practices.

A crucial element to effective use of formative assessment data is to ensure all personnel have a common understanding of key terms and concepts. Unfortunately, this understanding appears to be erroneously assumed but not actually practiced. We discovered this for ourselves when we studied DBDM terminology and alignment of definitions between teachers and school level administrators. Through our research with a small group of elementary schools, we discovered a 50% disconnect between how principal and assistant principals defined **key** terms used on a daily or weekly basis regarding assessment and accountability from the teachers in the same schools. This was a shocking discovery for the research team and why we have integrated vocabulary alignment activities in our own personal work with schools. An essential early step in promoting the data literacy and the collaborative culture necessary for successful implementation of the formative assessment cycle is to ensure all staff members have a uniform understanding of the data terminology utilized. Without this your professional development efforts will not be successful.

Through our research, we have developed a sense-making process school leaders can use to identify any potential concerns related to misunderstandings of data terminology. We have found this to be a useful tool in our work in the schools. Once your school staff has a common understanding of the data language you are speaking, the formative DBDM process is much easier to implement. This process is found in the Worksheet section of this book.

Now that we have reviewed the principles of formative assessment, we transition to the cycle of formative DBDM.

The Cycle of Formative Data Based Decision Making

3 | Introducing the Cycle

In the previous chapters of this book, we discussed the importance of DBDM and its links to formative assessment and instruction. We have asserted formative DBDM is a complementary set of skills that go to the heart of the instructional core. We have also discussed how formative assessment is essential to progressive pedagogy—you cannot implement meaningful or effective formative DBDM systems without a strong connection to its primary links to instruction. This is not about moving student groups around but is about all members of the learning community clarifying their goals, assessing their progress towards those goals, and self-monitoring and adjusting behaviors because of these self-assessments.

In this section of the book, each chapter outlines step-by-step strategies school leaders can implement to be more effective at formative data based decision making. We lay out a cycle of improvement drawn from our experiences working with teachers and school leaders in the areas of formative assessment and DBDM. Perhaps the most valuable thing we have learned is that growth and improvement is built incrementally from:

1. **small successes.**
2. **setting goals.**
3. **assessing progress.**
4. **self-monitoring and self-adjusting to better achieve the goal.**

The aim is to build organizational capacity to sustain the effort. Contextualized examples provided by leaders facilitating the process are an important way to model small steps towards a larger goal. These steps exemplify key aspects of the change or growth you want to achieve helping to

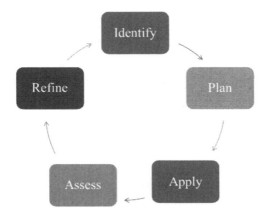

Figure 3.1 Cycle of Formative Data Based Decision Making

teach the organization to sustain the desired change. In the previous chapter, we discussed the importance of bringing in contextualized examples as you introduce and use this cycle. These examples are important for teachers to "see" how to implement the steps of the cycle. The suggested iterative cycle involves evaluating need and identifying existing information, developing an actionable plan, putting the plan into motion, assessing progress, and making refinements based on what was learned so far (see Figure 3.1). We fully explore this cycle in the remaining chapters of this book.

An Overview of the Cycle of Formative Data Based Decision Making

Identify

The first step in our model is designed to examine your school's data to determine patterns in student errors and misconceptions and possible gaps between what was assessed and what was taught. Initially this should be a macro view, looking for general trends in the data. This macro view is essential to establishing and refining a global understanding of the relationship between students' measured performance and instruction. Part of the evaluation of school- and grade-level data should look at not only patterns or trends within specific subject areas but also for potential concerns that run consistently among different subject areas and/or across grade levels.

Plan

During this step, teachers work to identify their own specific learning intentions based on the curriculum and on their own instructional needs. Teachers work in smaller teams to understand the nature of the standards-based learning objectives, which are often written in a technical way and can require this deconstruction to provide clarity regarding the goals of the objective.

Apply

In the Apply step of the model teachers carry out the collaboratively designed lesson plans and utilize a number of formative assessment practices designed to engage students in the learning process in deeper, more substantive ways than is typically the case. An important part of the Apply step is built-in opportunities for teachers and instructional leaders to reflect on observed changes in student interactions in the classroom: potential changes in engagement with the content, their classmates, and the teacher. Although test scores can reveal important information about student progress, they do not help educators recognize changes/improvement in the affective domains of learning.

Assess

The next step of the model provides the vital link to all the preceding steps by gathering empirical evidence of the impact of the evaluation of previous data, the identification of targeted areas of focus, and the associated planning and application of instructional and assessment strategies. During this step, teachers and instructional leaders are able to ascertain which aspects of their planning and implementation were effective, which showed promise, and which seemed to miss the mark. Here, the data team collaboratively looks at test score data; other evidence of student performance, as well as their reflective logs; and builds the next iteration from a strengthened platform of success.

Refine

The last step is closely tied to the assessment of impact, but looks to future implementations and gathers lessons learned from all stakeholders and at all steps of the model. This feedback capitalizes on success and mitigates weaknesses by only promoting what was effective to subsequent iterations of the process. During this step, we catalogue lessons learned, a sort of locally produced and contextually relevant "What Works Clearinghouse" of effective practices. Cataloging effective practices links changes in student learning with instruction and builds internal capacity, professional confidence, and trust in team members. We would argue this will increase motivation, professional respect, and buy-in to the model and, in turn, will stabilize the teachers' workforce.

Deep Alignment: Linking Learning and Teaching

One of the key elements of our model is the development of deep pedagogical alignment between student performance data and instruction. **Deep Pedagogical Alignment** is the degree to which instructional methods outlined in lesson plans and then carried out in the classroom ensures that students will learn and retain information. We are all well acquainted with alignment, linking what is tested with the written and taught curriculum. Clearly this is important; if we do not teach what is measured or measure what we teach, then the result will not be valid. However, **alignment at this basic level does not do much to improve teaching or learning.** It merely assures we are measuring the same things covered in the curriculum (see Figure 3.2). This level of alignment addresses the issue of test validity, but on its own says nothing about instruction. It does not address the types of learning experiences students are having in the classroom that will lead to deep, substantive learning.

The next layer of alignment needs to be Deep Pedagogical Alignment. As stated earlier and reinforced here: This is the degree to which instructional methods outlined in lesson plans are carried out in the classroom

Figure 3.2 Basic Model of Alignment

and **will ensure** students will learn and retain information at the appropriate cognitive level. If the teaching methods rely primarily on direct expository instruction to passive learners, students are unlikely to retain information beyond the short-cycle classroom assessments. Here we see gaps between grade-level and district quarterly assessments as well as state assessments. In a nutshell, the first layer of alignment we are all familiar with addresses content validity. This alone does not address instruction.

Deep Pedagogical Alignment

In order to get at deep pedagogical alignment that will promote real improvements in learning you need to integrate pedagogy and learning into the model (see Figure 3.2). Without this, you cannot address the quality and/or effectiveness of the curriculum, instruction, and student learning behaviors. **Without addressing pedagogy in questions about alignment, you cannot make sound data based decisions.** As you will see in the following sections that outline the cycle of formative DBDM, the infusion of pedagogy plays a central role in the model that allows school leaders and teachers to better understand students' misconceptions and possible instructional deficits. This in turn provides better grounding to make effective adjustments to instruction. The worksheet **Deep Alignment: Linking Learning and Teaching** provides teachers with a detailed description of the issue and challenges of alignment, followed by a process for thinking through how to assure that there is appropriate alignment between the standard, the implied or stated level of cognitive complexity and the associated instructional practices.

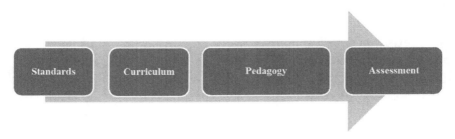

Figure 3.3 Deep Instructional Alignment Model

The Most Fundamental Form of Assessment is Self-Assessment

Finally, before we move to the steps within the model itself, we want to emphasize the centrality of **self-assessment** in all quality assessment programs. All assessments ultimately need to become some form of self-assessment in order to have an impact on learning. If assessment feedback is not reflected on, weighed, or considered in some manner, then it serves no purpose. Consider the student who has a math quiz returned, looks at it briefly to see the grade, and tucks it inside a textbook or throws it out. In this example, the lack of self-assessment of performance on the quiz renders the formative nature of the quiz ineffectual. Essentially, the student is not able to consider his or her strengths and weaknesses on the skills assessed and consider where needed to strengthen future performance. In the same way, if teachers and school leaders do not self-assess the meaning of student performance data in reference to their roles within the school, the explanatory potential of those data will not be revealed, and the patterns of instructional deficits will be allowed to continue.

Self-assessment for students means being **active agents in their own learning,** and for teachers it means monitoring and adjusting their instructional practices to better meet students' needs, that is, being active agents in their own professional growth.

Active Involvement of Stakeholders

One of the most important aspects about effective formative uses of assessment information is that stakeholders are actively involved in giving meaning to data. Other people's assessments have little impact compared to self-assessment. Self-assessments allow a person's judgments of assessment feedback to alter the individual's behavior accordingly (metacognition). Assessment will only have an impact on an individual's behavior if that person internalizes it in some way; if it does not become a form of self-assessment, then it is often simply disregarded. You need to view all assessment design from the following standpoint: Will the student, the teacher, or the school leader use the assessment in some form or another to *self-assess*?

Assessment Should Foster Independence

What we mean by this is the ability to utilize feedback to assess strengths and weaknesses and to make appropriate adjustments to behavior. However, many current assessment practices can actually foster dependence, in which student performance data are analyzed by data teams or are otherwise removed from the teachers who will ultimately have to act on this assessment information. At the students' level, students often look to the assessment for judgments about their performance, basically putting themselves in our hands. This removes them from the responsibility for monitoring their own progress and fosters dependence. A central question school leaders should ask themselves is, How are the people at the different levels of the school organization self-assessing in relationship to student performance data?

And this leads to a central tenet that needs to be integrated into the formative DBDM process—allowing students to be actively engaged in the cycle of formative DBDM. Much of what we talk about in this book is how *school leaders* can lead a formative DBDM process. We talk some about the classroom processes, but more from a leadership standpoint. Keep in mind that without allowing students, ultimately, to be active agents in their own learning, this process will not be implemented with fidelity. Adult learning theory informs us that teachers need to see the "fit" of a PD activity into their own classrooms (Langer, 2000). The same is true for students—you need to make instruction and learning relevant and meaningful. Part of making instruction and the content meaningful to students is allowing them to be a part of the process—helping to determine their own learning goals and assess their own progress.

Researchers have pointed out that significant learning gains occur when

- formative assessment begins with offering students a clear picture of learning intentions.
- students receive feedback on their work that helps them understand where they are with respect to the desired learning intention.
- students engage in self-assessment.
- formative assessment provides an understanding of specific steps that students can take to improve. (Chappuis, 2005)

If you took a learning walk in your school and spoke with students, would they be able to

- tell you specifically what they were learning?
- tell you what strategies they were using to accomplish that learning?
- explain what tools they are using to monitor their progress?
- tell you how they knew they had accomplished that learning and to what degree?
- tell you what they needed to do to close learning gaps?
- *and* explain how much learning is under their control?

Although the preceding components are beyond the purview of this book in terms of leading your staff through a formative DBDM process, these tenets must be kept at the forefront of your conversations. Throughout the formative DBDM cycle, continually reference back to how students are being engaged in the process.

4 | Identify

Identify—essentially a macro data review—is the first step in the cycle of formative DBDM. The goal of this step of the cycle is to identify, through a schoolwide review of data, the key school improvement foci that will give clear direction and emphasis to the subsequent steps in the process. You will then use the broader school learning intentions as you meet with teams to identify their specific team-level (content, grade, etc.) learning intentions. In our view this is a critical step, because it provides the school leader a data informed, big-picture view of where the school is along with the central areas that will be targeted during the improvement process. With this broad, global perspective, school leaders are better prepared to guide overall school improvement planning and to facilitate more focused subject-area and grade-level team efforts. Without such a perspective to guide formative DBDM, a school's data informed efforts may lack focus and direction.

Collaboration and Decision Making—Striking a Balance

This step poses several challenges in finding the right balance between collaborative decision making and the need to make clear and decisive decisions. We strongly advocate for all school staff to be involved in the utilization of data to make decisions around school improvement and the instructional direction. If you leave people out of the process, there is no sense of buy-in or of affiliation with the overall plan, and the fidelity of the strategies will be compromised. However, the reality is not everyone can, or should, be involved in every facet of the decision-making process because of factors such as time and other organizational resource limitations, as well the systems perspectives of the leadership team versus the classroom teachers' perspectives. During the Identify step of the cycle, school leaders need to guide the collaborative process in such a way that brings teacher voices and perspectives into the decision making process while balancing other factors including district and state level requirements and pressures. You need to provide a starting point that identifies the primary areas of content and/or instructional focus or, as we have called them, "learning intentions."

Creating a Climate of Psychological Safety and Innovation

A careful review of a school's multiple forms of data about teaching and learning can be intimidating and can require a degree of risk taking for teachers. When you peel back these layers of what is really happening in terms of teaching and student learning you are likely to have potentially uncomfortable discoveries and conversations. There are interpersonal risks inherent in formative DBDM that need to be managed to ensure both individual and organizational learning and growth. Some organizational psychologists refer to this as psychological safety (Edmondson 1999, 2002), which has been described as "the degree to which people perceive their work environment as conducive to taking these interpersonal risks" (Edmondson, 2002, p. 5). There is a great deal of variation in people's willingness to participate in activities when the outcomes are uncertain, as well as those activities that may be harmful to how they are perceived within the organization (Edmondson, 2002). The organizational climate can have a large impact on whether people are willing to take risks and approach situations where the outcomes are uncertain.

A formative DBDM process requires everyone in the school organization to face potential change, uncertainty, and ambiguity. This is crucial during the Identify step. When you begin peeling back the layers of your data to discover the root causes of a particular issue, you do not always know what you will find. Engaging in formative DBDM requires participants to ask questions, to probe individual and organizational assumptions, to seek advice or help, to seek outside perspectives, and to try new ideas. Although all these behaviors are related to your goals of collaboration, innovation, and improved performances (Edmondson 1999; West 2000), they nonetheless ask participants to take a certain amount of risk to their psychological safety.

Creating a psychologically safe climate can stimulate innovation (West & Anderson, 1996) as well as aid in the integration of these innovations (D'Andrea-O'Brien & Buono, 1996). This in turn creates a challenging set of circumstances for you to manage; you are asking the school community to engage in something challenging and uncertain while at the same time helping to establish a school climate that mitigates individuals' and groups' aversion to risk taking. During this process you need to be particularly sensitive to this because people are more risk aversive in the presence of their supervisors. You should work to mitigate risks to support individual and group learning, create a structure that provides safe boundaries for learning, and emphasize innovation.

Classroom Observation Tools

The pressures of standards, assessments, and accountability can influence schools to "teach to the test" and to rely too heavily on the instructional and assessment approaches most expedient in "covering" the standards. We know from our earlier discussion these "conduits of pressure" (Mintrop & Trujillo, 2005) to raise test scores can shape instruction and overshadow our significant knowledge about how children learn. Unfortunately, what is efficient in terms of covering the standards does not actually translate to long-term and transferable learning. As part of a comprehensive data informed school-improvement effort, collecting information on the types of instructional and assessment practices utilized, as well as the kind of learning interactions student have in classrooms, will help to better align standard driven goals with the instructional and assessment strategies research has demonstrated promotes learning.

We have developed two tools to guide school leaders through the process of assessing their school's instructional climate and gain both schoolwide and more focused classroom perspectives. The schoolwide tool **Factors that Influence Learning Observation Tool** draws from John Hattie's (2013) *Visible Learning* book that synthesizes research on a wide range of factors that influence learning. This tool uses a summary list of these influential factors along with their effectiveness. School leaders can use this tool to better understand the factors with the greatest impact on learning. This provides important data to establish the macro understanding of the school's instructional climate. Supporting these observations with a more focused evaluation of the classroom level is the **How Children Learn**

Classroom Observation Tool. This tool uses Vosniadou's (2001, 2003) *How Children Learn*, which synthesizes the learning sciences literature on universal aspects of how children learn. Using this tool, school leaders can collect information about the degree to which these various learning science factors are present in classroom. Because of the comprehensiveness of this tool, it is unlikely that you will observe all of these factors in a single classroom visit. You and your team may want to strategically focus on one to three areas in a given visit.

These two tools can provide your team with a means of gaining greater understanding about the instructional climate of the school. Along with the review of student performance data and the multiple measures of school data, your team will be able to develop a comprehensive and balanced outlook of the school, positioning yourselves to more effectively facilitate the next steps in the cycle.

Creating a Structure for Reviewing Data and Identifying Core Issues

As we discussed earlier in this book, we are inundated with data. Schools, leaders, and teachers have volumes of data to review. This can become overwhelming, and we have seen educators essentially "shut down" data overload. In the Identify step of the cycle the leadership team is responsible for a large-scale data review to identify the primary areas of focus—the overall school learning intentions. In this book, we cannot tell you what your particular school's learning intentions will be—each are school-site specific. And it may be the case that as your building staff become more comfortable with this process, more teachers will become involved in the Identify component of the cycle. This becomes more commonplace for schools that have implemented high functioning learning communities.

There is no one "right way" to approach the use of data in your school's decision-making cycle. What is critical is that you and your team commit to a process and help the school and that teachers identify the school level learning intentions. From there, you can drill down to the classroom level to develop classroom (and/or content) learning intentions. During the Identify step of the process, you will conduct an overall review of the school's data looking for schoolwide themes or patterns that may reveal broader areas of focus for the overall improvement effort.

Identifying Sources of Schoolwide Data for Review

What Data Can and Cannot Tell Us

Before we can talk about identifying sources of data for the macro view, we should briefly clarify what the most commonly available and used forms of data can and cannot tell us. One of the ideas we have tried to make clear in this book is not all data is informative and any individual source of data only tells a portion of the story. It can be intimidating to look at printouts of large volumes of data. Questions arise, such as "What do we focus on?" and "How do we bring actionable meaning to our interpretations?"

If you look at a given set of assessment data, you need to consider the following as a team:

- What do the data tell us about our students' learning, including about their motivation, understanding of learning goals, and their prior knowledge or level of engagement?

- What do our data tell us about the kinds of instructional practices that were utilized?

Most assessment data are reasonable approximations of where students are on a discrete standard or set of standards. As discussed in Chapter 1, much of the data you do have access to are simply outcome data, that is, common assessments, benchmark tests, and end-of-year tests. These kinds of data by themselves do not go very far in terms of informing us about the process of learning. They have limited utility for the kind of DBDM that we are focusing on in this book. We have provided a tool—**Identifying Data to Make Decisions**—that assists your team in evaluating the utility of data in your formative DBDM process in a rational way that helps to address the safe psychological and innovative climate we espouse are important in this cycle.

Establish a Process of Analyzing and Interpreting the Data

It is important to link instructional goals with the review of student performance data. This provides an instructional context to the data. Without this you cannot assess data in instructionally meaningful ways. Failing to link instructional goals with student performance data can also lead to the common mistake of grouping and regrouping students by performance levels without looking at the potential instructional deficits that may account for lower student performance. You cannot assess student performance data in a vacuum and should iteratively examine student learning progress compared to articulated learning intentions. Then readjust instruction to meet student learning needs.

During the Identify step you need to do the following:

1. Carefully assess the learning intention that was taught.

2. Investigate to see if there are any concerns regarding alignment between the written and the taught curriculum.

3. Evaluate available data on student performance to better understand any student misconceptions and possible instructional deficits (i.e., learning experiences that are not aligned with the cognitive level of the standard, a gap in alignment between the taught and tested curriculum, an emphasis on a departmental planning strategy in which one person on a team is responsible for planning for one standard and another is responsible for a second, etc.).

There are many different entry points into the Identify step where you and your leadership team work to assess the goal of what was taught and instructional concerns and to identify the two to three school-learning intentions (or whatever your school has determined to be as the number of global school-learning intentions). This is where we cannot provide a lockstep prescription to your particular school context. You should examine your school district's expectations in terms of data utilization, use of district created curriculum resources and instructional models, the available multiple measures of data, what is missing, and what you need to gather. It is also important to reflect on your leadership team's background knowledge and skills around formative DBDM. Where is the team comfortable starting? What do they need to know to help understand the instructional context of the data you are reviewing?

Types of Data

We want to provide your team a starting point when considering the types of data you have available to conduct this macro review. We advocate for you to encourage your team leaders to brainstorm the types of data available using the multiple measures of data we discussed earlier in this book. What types of demographic data, process data, achievement data, and perception data are available? The data you review should provide different perspectives of achievement, and you should be careful to avoid an overemphasis on testing and accountability outcome data. Testing and accountability data does not inform the team *what* is happening in the classroom, and you could end up developing learning intentions that do not reflect the true learning needs of your students. In the following, we provide some initial suggestions for your data collection:

- Samples of student work
- Formative classroom assessments
- Teacher observations
- Teachers' lesson plans
- Team, department, or grade-level documents (notes, plans, goals)
- Student feedback
- Portfolios
- Surveys—students, teachers, or any of the key stakeholders in the school community
- Attendance patterns for the school, grade levels, and teachers
- Photographs of student work (can reveal patterns of student engagement and time on task)
- Classroom videos of instruction
- Student self-reflections and feedback
- Parent reflections and feedback

Unpacking

One way of capturing the deeper instructional context of student performance data is to **unpack,** or deconstruct the standards being measured. We have provided a tool in the third part of this book that will help you guide your team through this process: **Unpacking Standards to Create Sound Learning Intentions.** This is a powerful tool that can be used both at the larger macro view in the Identify step and in turn in a more targeted way with grade-level and/or content teams. One way of thinking about unpacking is as a means of interrogating the assumptions you may have about student performance or other sources of data. Here you are unpacking the various elements of data by asking, "What is going on under the surface?" or "What is driving these outcomes?"

One of the approaches to the unpacking strategy we have used widely in our work is to carefully examine the learning standards (state, national, etc.) to be clearer about the goals, level of rigor, and the type of thinking processes and necessary instructional strategies. We review the language in the standards for the data we so we can have a deeper understanding of what exactly was assessed and clarify the types of knowledge called for in those standards. It is important for teachers to have a clear understanding why this strategy is important and effective. In our experiences, teachers can fall into the trap of using a district's pacing guide as the sole document to plan for instruction and to create assessments. As previously noted, one pitfall with the overreliance on the pacing guide for planning is that teachers will frequently create lessons not aligned at the content and cognitive levels. Unpacking can help teachers avoid this problem and focus on deep pedagogical alignment.

Determine Student Error Patterns

Next, you must evaluate your school's data to determine patterns in student errors and misconceptions, as well as any possible gaps between what was tested and what was taught. Initially this should be a macro view, looking for general data trends. You will find different themes emerge from this review. This macro view is essential to establishing and refining a global understanding of the relationship between students' measured performance and classroom instruction. Part of this evaluation of school- and grade-level data should look not only for patterns or trends within specific subject area but also for potential concerns that run consistently among different subject areas and/or across grade levels. (Keep in mind that although this macro view is important, classroom instruction is where the action is for improving student performance!) The following are examples of potential themes that may emerge. These are only five examples of any number of themes your own team may find:

- Data revealed a pattern of instructional strategies that were primarily at the lower end of Bloom's Taxonomy.

- Standards have been "covered" in most cases through carefully following pacing guides, but the integration of standards, both within the various subject areas and among them, is currently ignored. Time limitations are often the primary reason cited for this problem.

- Much of the process-oriented data collected (lesson plans, curriculum, etc.) revealed students often play a passive role in learning.

- Students are typically not involved in formatively utilizing assessment information to guide their learning and help develop strong metacognitive strategies.

- A review of teacher observations by the school's administrative team reveals little evidence of written feedback provided to teachers that speaks to the alignment of the written and the taught curriculum or that the learning experiences delivered during a lesson were at the appropriate cognitive level to match the standard or essential skill.

Other Activities to Help Identify Trends and Themes

We readily acknowledge that each school is unique and that not all tools work for all schools. We have provided a number of tools you can use throughout this step in the cycle, as well as throughout all steps in this book, to support your formative DBDM efforts.

Data Wall

The Data Wall has become standard practice in many schools. It is a good tool to visually sort through the clutter of data and can be used effectively during a number of steps of the cycle outlined in this book. During the Identify step, the data wall strategy can be used to collaboratively identify the central topics or themes that will give shape to the continued school improvement efforts. We have developed **The Data Wall: Data That Sticks** tool instructional leaders can use or adapt to guide the process. The idea of the data wall exercise is to pinpoint one area of focus for a teacher or administrator when trying to increase student achievement. This activity is interactive and visual. It walks participants through data clutter, weeds out items they cannot change swiftly, and helps them focus on one or two actions to take in order to tackle a problem.

Assessing the Conditions for Fostering the Development of the Whole Child

As discussed elsewhere in this book, the pressures to chase assessment measures and teach to the test can actually deflect your efforts from your goals. A narrow focus on delivering content in lockstep with pacing guides and other prescriptive processes can undermine the goal of real learning. As Blank and Berg (2006) emphasized, lasting and transferable learning involves multiple and interconnected domains and ignoring one that has an impact on all of them. We have utilized Blank and Berg's *6 Conditions for Fostering the Development of the Whole Child* to develop the **Assessing the Conditions for Fostering the Development of the Whole Child** tool for your team to ask themselves: What do our data tell us about the conditions needed to foster the development of the whole child? Briefly, these six areas are the instructional program; students' level of motivation; the physical, mental, and emotional health of the students; the climate of mutual respect and collaboration among the various stakeholders in the school community; community engagement; and the presence of high-quality early childhood development programs. This tool provides a means of assessing what a school's data can and cannot tell us about these factors, which in turn can help avoid the challenges of goal displacement (Blau & Scott, 1962).

The Problem Statement

Writing a brief yet descriptive statement that clearly identifies the central area or areas of concern will help to give focus to each of the data teams who will explore these issue at the more micro level. The following may be an example:

A comprehensive review of a variety of sources of evidence revealed concerns at both the instructional and the student level. Instructionally, there appears to be a lack of engaging students in more rigorous activities at the higher levels of Bloom's Taxonomy, and as such, students often have fewer opportunities to be active agents in their own learning. Data also suggested that students are struggling in two critical areas: reading comprehension and place value, fractions, and decimals.

This is essentially a problem statement that, in many cases, can easily be strategically linked to other similar documents such as school-improvement documents and mission statements. The added benefit of writing this document is you or your leadership team can assess the strategic alignment of your review of data with other improvement efforts. Where there is a lack of congruence, you will want to explore where and why these disconnects are occurring and work toward realigning your efforts.

Establishing a macro view of student performance provides a big picture framework for more detailed and actionable data based decision making. Grounded in a clearer understanding of the interrelationships among weaker and stronger areas of student performance you can then take narrower, subject area examinations of specific learning objectives. Once you have identified overarching schoolwide learning intentions you then want to move beyond a general view of student performance data and set short-term goals at the team, content, and/or grade level, identifying specific learning intentions and associated instructional and assessment strategies to focus on in subsequent parts of the model. Having modeled the process at the school level, you can ask department chairs, team leaders, or data coaches to facilitate a similar process (while keeping in mind the need to involve school leaders throughout the process). This is important because the macro view established in the Identify step grounds the school community in the more pressing and global issues, and then you drill down to the content, team, or grade level to look more deeply at the factors among teachers in smaller groups who can take specific actions.

One of the challenges department and grade-level teams can encounter in evaluating their own data is the inherent risk involved in asking the deeper questions about why students may be struggling in certain areas. Just as the broader school-level review of data can evoke uncertainty and discomfort, the more detailed team-level analysis can be that much more uncomfortable as it can begin to feel much more personal. Teachers' psychological safety can be at stake, and team facilitators need to be sensitive to these issues. Although this is important at the school level, it becomes far more pointed at the smaller team level as teachers' strengths and weaknesses become far more apparent when thoroughly unpacking our data. Although school leaders will need to feel welcome to join these groups, it may be important to be particularly thoughtful in monitoring one's behaviors in these meetings and considering the factors outlined previously that can contribute to mitigating psychological risk for teachers. All members of the school leadership team should work with grade-level/content leaders and department chairs to help them learn and strengthen their skills as facilitating formative DBDM activities.

5 | Plan

Once the school leadership team has identified one or more specific learning intentions for a select grade level and/or department, the school's leaders will want to work with the teaching staff to begin planning for instruction. The recommendation is to begin this work with a smaller group of faculty. For example, perhaps the math strand of Measurement & Geometry has continued to surface as an area for improvement when examining summative achievement results in Grade 4 over the last 2 school years. As a result, the leadership team has decided that working with this grade level, on this particular math strand, will be a priority for the first semester of the school year.

It is important to note it is not realistic to expect administrators to plan for instruction in every classroom and with every teacher—nor would they want to. This book is written for school personnel who are *leading* the formative DBDM process. Each classroom is unique; each teacher and instructional style different—and you do not want to get to a rote process in which all instruction looks the same, regardless of the students and the teacher. Rather, you want to respect the differences from classroom to classroom, help teachers understand the learning intentions, develop meaningful learning intentions for their own classrooms, and help teachers understand how to plan an approach that fully incorporates the use of data in formative ways to make ongoing instructional improvements.

Remember, your staff may be at different levels of understanding regarding using data to make ongoing instructional decisions and in effectively utilizing formative assessments. Be cognizant that as you progress, you may need to make adjustments based on the experience and knowledge of your teachers. **The Level of Understanding of Components of Effective Assessment Tool** in Part III can be used by school administrators to help determine teachers' level of comfort and understanding regarding some of the key components of effective assessment.

You need to decide how you are going to approach the planning process. It is critical that you outline this approach prior to implementing it (and we recommend you do this for each step of the cycle—as you would expect a good teacher to have a written lesson plan, this process requires you to commit your processes to paper and understand fully what is involved at each step). We recommend engaging your leadership team around how you are going to work on this step of the cycle. Write down your ideas about how to work with your staff. Some leadership teams we have worked with have taken one of the learning intentions identified as an area for improvement and created a template for grade levels and/or departments to use as a guide when beginning this work. In this scenario, time was spent outlining a process that could be used as a model to guide a team of teachers. Such a resource builds confidence and helps ensure fidelity to the process created by the leadership team. As a part of this process, it was also important for teachers on these teams to have a clear understanding of the purpose of this work and the research to support it. Even when given a road map to follow, it is important to know why you are headed in a certain direction.

As noted earlier, to ensure staff understands this process, it will be integral to the success of this initiative to provide PD in smaller group settings. In our experiences, we found that implementation pitfalls are reduced significantly when teachers are able to engage in a dialogue about this work. Although we agree that all faculty need to be introduced to this work as part of an intentional process, this does not mean it has to occur at the same time. Those schools with strong learning community structures, however, could find great benefit in a working faculty meeting in which content and/ or grade levels are processed through in small groups, whereas in a larger venue, the initial questions and processes to addressing the learning intentions in their own classrooms.

Change

There is something very important we want to discuss at the planning step. Many of you reading this may already understand the change process. And if that is the case, feel free to skip over this section. However, even if you are a master at organizational change, we think it is still good to keep in mind some central tenants when implementing any new process, program, structure, innovation, or something that is "different" into your school.

Where is your school in relation to understanding and effectively using formative assessment practices as a regular part of instruction? If your answer is not very far, you are looking at a second-order change initiative. If most of your teachers are generally comfortable with formative assessment practices and do this naturally, and you are looking to integrate a more formal structure to this process, then perhaps you are more at a first-order level change.

We hear quite a bit about first- and second-order change in schools. First-order change is change that tends to be more in line with the school's typical norms. This type of change does not "upset the apple cart," and once introduced, you are fairly certain that it will be generally embraced and accepted into the school's structure. Second-order change goes against the status quo, is uncomfortable, and requires a deep investment in time and effort in order for the initiative to take root. You need to know what level of change you are implementing in your school when engaging in the formative data base decision-making process. If you do not know, then your implementation of the formative DBDM cycle will probably not be implemented with fidelity. This is because any good leader needs to know at what point your organization is in terms of readiness for change and needs for implementing something new. We argue that you need to know the readiness of your staff before you start working with your leadership team at the Identify step. However, we feel that this is the most critical section of the book to talk about what type of change process you are going to encounter and factors to consider when implementing this cycle.

Earlier in this book, we talked about barriers to the effective implementation of a DBDM process. Understanding the barriers will help you with this process and effectively working with your teachers. Although identifying any potential barriers to the successful implementation of the cycle, you should also assess whether this process will be a first- or a second-order change initiative.

In this section we are talking about planning—and you are asking your teachers to plan in ways that may be qualitatively different from how they used to plan. No longer are you asking them to assess at the end of their lessons in summative forms as the sole means of understanding if their students "got" the lesson. You are working with your leadership team to facilitate an instructional process that integrates a variety of ongoing assessment techniques that are integrated into instruction—in essence, you are asking teachers to no longer think about instruction and assessment as separate and discrete components. And this may represent a significant deviation from what they are used to. It may be the case that your teachers are already on board with this approach, and this process will be easier for you to implement. In some schools we have worked with, administrators and school leadership teams have identified "model teachers" who have served in a coach capacity to colleagues. In one district, two schools worked together to identify best practices surrounding formative assessment in their respective schools, and the staffs met on a quarterly basis to share ideas.

We want to emphasize this process is **deliberate and intentional.** And it will take time. There is no actual magic solution that is a quick, one-size cure-all for addressing instructional gaps in student performance and that will help "fix" classroom challenges. However, if you implement this cycle in a deliberate and intentional way, with a clear understanding of your staff's starting point, we do believe you will find this process will help support a transformation in instructional practice.

Alignment

After you have worked with your leadership team to identify the processes needed to implement the planning cycle with your staff, you will transition to focusing on the learning intentions. At this point, you need to make sure you fully understand the nature of the learning intentions and ensure the instruction will align with essential knowledge and skills at both the content and the cognitive level. A common mistake that principals and assistant principals make is they often leave this work up to a lead teacher, a coach, or a department chair. It will be important for your teachers to see the principal and assistant principal or principals displaying this level of knowledge and this skill set. Although no one is expecting the leaders to memorize standards, they need to be able to create an organized system allowing leaders to quickly retrieve any essential skills within a given standard. Creating such a system on your computer or mobile device is time well spent, because this resource will become important during the observation process when you are looking to provide teachers with written feedback regarding alignment. In a larger district we worked with, curriculum leaders created this resource for the district's building administrators. Feedback, particularly from secondary administrators who are tasked with observing such courses as chemistry, was that this resource proved to be invaluable.

When beginning conversations with teachers about alignment while discussing formative assessment, it is important to keep in mind we are not just talking about alignment between the taught and tested curriculum. We have found in our work there is sometimes a significant disconnect between what is taught in the classrooms and what is articulated in the written curriculum. Part of this appears to come from confusion around standards-based learning objectives, and some of this comes from teachers relying on the "old playbook" that was used in previous years. In our experience, another significant factor to ensuring tight alignment between the written and taught curriculum is to clearly communicate your expectations to teachers that lesson plans and learning experiences must be derived from this written resource. In some schools we have worked with, this is done through the staff handbook and is reiterated during every postobservation conference. For example, a frequently asked question to a novice teacher during a postobservation conference could be, "Talk to me about what resources you use to plan for instruction. How do you ensure tight alignment between the written curriculum and your lessons?"

We have found that standards-based learning objectives are often written in very technical terms. Although the authors of the standards (Common Core and/or state) understand what they are trying to convey in the very technical standards document, many teachers have a difficult time deciphering the instructional expectations required to meet the written standards. We see this, too, in district curricula. One of the concerns is that these documents remove students from the instructional process—it seems as though in these documents, students are seen as passive recipients of instruction who are not engaged in the instructional process itself in these standards. Although the standards discuss the student's mastery of an objective, this often appears to be as far as most standards-based objectives get in terms of the *student's* involvement in the process. Remember we are emphasizing the need to fully integrate students into the formative assessment process. We want to make sure students know what the learning intentions are for the day's lesson and understand the expectations and success criteria. Often, the standards-based objectives are very abstract and are written in a manner that is hard to understand at the macro level by students (and others). These standards are not written in terms that easily allow teachers to think about the instructional processes that are involved to meet the standard either.

As leaders, you need to help teachers in the planning step of the formative DBDM process to **deconstruct** the standards. This is critical to effectively planning their instruction and to integrating formative assessments into their lessons, rather than summative assessments, which is often the case. Deconstructing standards help teachers and students to be clear on the goals of the objective/learning intention. To do this you "unpack" the objective, outlining its essential features and write, what we call "learning intentions." We initially discussed learning intentions in the Identify step of the cycle. During the Identify step you were identifying the macro level school learning intentions. Here you are drilling down to the content/team and teacher levels. The **learning intentions** provide plain-language, operational, learning goals that offer greater clarity than is generally the case with the standards based objectives. Additionally, you use this plain-language goal to write **"I can" statements.** Students can then use the "I can" statements as a self-assessment tool as they progress toward mastery of the learning objectives.

We have provided several tools to help you guide your staff through this process. The **Lesson Plan/Assessment Preparation Form** is designed to assist teachers as they work in a collaborative manner to determine what learning experiences will be provided to students during a particular unit of study. We have provided different tools that can assist you and your team as you work with teachers to connect meaningful success criteria with the identified learning intentions. The **Learning Intentions and Success Criteria Planning Form** tool assists the team as they process through the specific standards that are required by the state and/or curriculum guide, the essential learning intentions, the level or levels of cognitive demand and determining success criteria written in the form of "I can" statements. Associated with this worksheet are two examples that we completed with schools during our work.

Another tool is the **Planning for Success** worksheet. We have found this tool to be beneficial as teams and teachers work collaboratively to become more familiar with such terms as *learning intentions* and *success criteria*. As noted earlier in the book, it is critical for all stakeholders to have the same operational definitions of the terminology. The Planning for Success worksheet helps to reinforce some of the key components to effective lesson planning. For example, this tool helps teachers to think more strategically about the creation of success criteria in order to ensure these are of high quality and are meaningful to both the learners and the teacher. This worksheet will also help teachers to identify higher order thinking activities and outcomes as a part of their lesson planning process.

One additional tool that we have created is designed to assist students with the monitoring of their progress as they work towards meeting or exceeding the success criteria during a unit of study. The **Student Monitoring**

Log should be completed by students and should be referenced during a unit. The log is an excellent tool for use by teachers during student conferences (formal or informal) to gauge student understanding at a given point in time, and it can be used by students during small groups to facilitate dialogue and reflection on their understanding of a specific learning intention. The Student Monitoring Log can also be used by students to prepare for both formative and summative assessments. For example, imagine the student who has several pages of logs and begins to prepare for an end of unit assessment. In addition to other materials, the logs will help the student to gauge just how prepared he is for this assessment, and it will serve as an excellent study guide. As noted earlier in the book, it is critical for students to have a clear understanding of the learning intentions and the success criteria for a unit of study. The Student Monitoring Log helps to ensure that students have this understanding and that they are actively involved in monitoring their progress. Note that although we use the terms *concrete*, *representational*, and *abstract*, you can and should use the language your school district uses to identify varied levels of learning thinking. We have provided two examples of how this tool has been used in Part III, as well.

We previously discussed the change process and potential barriers to change. To help facilitate overcoming these barriers we have developed a tool, modeled after Kagen and Lahey's (2009) immunity to change concept, designed to help your team identify underlying assumptions, organizational habits, and competing commitments that may interfere with achieving learning goals within your school. This tool provides a means to identify potential barriers and can create the needed clarity to overcome these barriers. Given the previous discussion about risk taking and psychological safety, school leaders should assure a safe setting for utilizing this tool.

Unpacking

Typically, when educators talk about unpacking learning standards, it is in terms of teachers clarifying the types of knowledge and skills called for in the standard. They then link the knowledge and skills to the unit or curriculum learning intentions, outlining objectives that include behaviors students will exhibit to show learning and the conditions under which the students will exhibit those behaviors. Teachers then outline the criteria (i.e., success criteria) used to determine whether learners have met the objective and develop authentic forms of assessing student mastery of the standard. We provide a number of tools you can use to guide your faculty through this process. You and your leadership team should identify the tools that fit your school the best and modify them to fit your particular needs. Each of the tools can be used with your teachers to drill down to the core learning intentions for their instructional units.

Although unpacking and identifying learning intentions are done initially during the Identify step at the macro level, unpacking and identifying the learning intentions are also important parts of the Plan step in the cycle. We have seen these planning activities carried out in a number of ways with faculty. Some administrators have selected standards that represent areas of improvement from the previous year's end-of-year assessments in one or more content areas. In a large- or small-group setting, teams of teachers work through the unpacking process to gain a better understanding of the steps involved as well as gain more familiarity with the standards deemed "essential" in the current school year's improvement plan. Other administrators will repeat this planning step at the end of each quarter, utilizing benchmark performance results. In this scenario, grade levels and/or departments will meet in teams, analyze data, and unpack the standards for skills that were frequently missed. We have worked with other schools that identify several standards that represent areas of focus for the year. Once unpacked, this information is then used to drive ongoing intervention and remediation efforts throughout the school year for these select skills.

We believe it is also important to reflect on the **degree to which these processes involve students** in setting goals, identifying strategies on how to reach goals, and assessment strategies to self-monitor while still learning. Our work has focused on adapting this strategy of scaffolding student goal setting and learning to address these issues and focuses back on our assertion of the importance of allowing students to be actively engaged in their own learning.

We contend without the added layer of the student's involvement in the planning step of this cycle any formative DBDM process will not be successful. We are certain you have seen this firsthand in your own schools. You have gone through a very carefully planned lesson, designed excellent research-based activities that you thought went very well, and then assessed only to find the students did not learn what you thought they would. Students must continually be involved in the process, and we believe all students at any grade level can have some degree of involvement. The same tools you use with your instructional staff throughout the cycle can also be adapted to use with students.

Defining Quality With Students

Another important aspect of the planning process related to unpacking and clarifying learning intentions is working with students to define quality. **When students clearly understand their learning goals, can define what quality work looks like, and self-assess based on the success criteria that has been clearly communicated, students perform at much higher levels.** What this describes are aspects of **self-regulated learning,** or what you might think about as an active orientation toward learning.

The more apt students have learned to apply these and other active strategies on their own, but as Mayer (2002) pointed out, the performance of less apt students can be increased to nearly the same level when these types of strategies are taught and the teacher provides scaffolding to support them. Struggling students benefit when you scaffold experiences that help them to be clear about learning goals and about what quality looks like in working toward the goal. These are preconditions to self-regulated learning.

Once you have unpacked the standard and communicated the connections between the lesson and the unit or the curriculum's learning intentions, students should have a clearer idea of the essential knowledge and skills for a given standard. Although this general learning intention is important, by itself, it does not provide enough detail for students to self-assess while they are still learning. Understanding, in more detail, what specific behaviors students will need to exhibit to show learning and the conditions under which the students will exhibit those behaviors is the next step. We are calling this ***defining quality.*** Although we are stressing the importance of having students do this, you should guide your teachers through this process first so they understand how to do it, as well as how they define quality.

After clarifying the learning goal, we need to work with students to establish what they would have to know and the criteria used to determine whether they are able to demonstrate mastery of the learning objective. In other words, **given the learning intention, what does quality work look like?** This is a challenge for many students, particularly lower performing students who have adopted a passive orientation toward learning.

Defining quality is akin to rubrics, which give clear criteria for what constitutes quality work. Defining quality is a broader concept for which rubrics are one way of a providing focus and clarity for students as they work toward the learning goal.

So, what does this look like in practice? This is dependent on the nature of the learning intention. Learning intentions that are primarily at the knowledge level, such as learning multiplication facts, will define quality differently than will learning the fundamentals of scientific reasoning. **Thoughtfully unpacking the standard and defining clearly the learning intention is critical to knowing how to define quality work.** Defining quality is also dependent on the types of activities one chooses to use. Although various activities are targeted at the learning intention, the definition of quality for writing assignments will be different from the definition of quality for oral presentations, for example.

One way of thinking about this is to view defining quality as a way to provide increasingly focused information to students for them to use to support their self-regulated learning:

- Clarify the learning intention.

- Define generally what constitutes quality work.

- Define quality in more specific, targeted ways on individual assignments.

- Select applicable high-impact strategies.

- Conduct formal or informal PD with internal or external resources.

- Collaboratively codesign the instructional intervention throughout the PD process.

Teacher involvement and feedback to staff are key components in selecting and successfully implementing high-impact strategies. It is important for teachers to have a voice and to play an active role in the practice of identifying high-yield strategies for use during instruction. In many schools we have worked with, this is done via the school leadership team and/or various grade levels/departments. In schools where this has worked well, teams have narrowed down to a list of three to five strategies and have made commitments to become well versed in these strategies. This is not to say that other strategies are not used, but the staff has made commitments to professional learning and to including these select strategies into their classrooms. This process brings a sense of ownership and group accountability for ensuring that "we are all growing together as professionals" in an effort to improve our instructional practices.

Administrators must provide feedback to staff about the implementation of the selected strategies in a supportive model of collegial supervision. Too many administrators and leadership teams are guilty of the "one-shot wonder" approach to PD and there is often very little follow up or feedback provided. In the successful schools we have visited, administrators make commitments to teachers to provide ongoing feedback. One administrator we know will conduct instructional walk-throughs on a regular basis and will provide feedback to staff on a particular high-impact strategy being emphasized in the school during a given quarter. The following week the administrator will include a brief overview in the weekly staff notice about all of the lessons observed (making general statements and not including teachers' names) using this strategy and will report the percentage of teachers whose work is "on target," as identified by the criteria set by school leadership team. As weeks pass, staff are able to see incremental gains in the percentage of on-target instruction for a given strategy. This same administrator has worked with her faculty to identify examples and non-examples of each high-impact strategy so that teachers were provided with a type of innovation configuration map that serves as a guide and as a constant reminder about how effective implementation looks for each high-impact strategy.

The culture of collaboration noted above is also frequently found in schools that collaboratively codesign the instructional intervention. One popular approach we have seen in successful schools has been the Lesson Study model (Wiburg & Brown, 2007). For example, in some schools we have worked with, the school leadership team has worked alongside grade levels and/or departments to identify select essential learning intentions that staff agreed would become the focus of the lesson study. In this protocol, teachers will collaboratively plan a lesson from the unpacking process through the design of the lesson to include the creation of the formative assessment or assessments. One teacher will volunteer to deliver the lesson to his or her class, while the other teachers on the team/department are in the room observing. Following the observation, the team debriefs to discuss all facets of the lesson. Adjustments are made, and the lesson is taught a second time to another group of students by another member of the team. (Some schools will repeat these steps one additional time.) In schools that have adopted this approach to address learning intentions that have repeatedly surfaced as areas for improvement as evidenced by lackluster student achievement results, you can imagine the level of knowledge and insight gained by teachers participating in this process. Although time intensive, it is our experience this particular model delivers results and helps to strengthen teachers' understanding of the content while sharpening a host of teaching skills.

Based on the nuances of a particular unpacked learning intention, you want to be strategic regarding the types of instructional practices (including formative assessment measures integrated into the instructional plan) you will utilize. This is important because it fosters the development of teachers' discretionary authority and provides the flexibility needed to meet the varying needs of students, teachers, classrooms, and schools. An important part of selecting the instructional practice or practices is challenging assumptions about teaching that can often lead to replicating approaches that were minimally effective in the first place. Throughout this step (and the cycle), capitalize on the various internal and external resources you have available to help teachers hone their pedagogical skills. Depending on the need, informal or formal PD can be organized to support teachers' implementation of the plans.

6 | Apply

The Apply step of the formative assessment leadership (FAL) cycle happens in the classroom. However, as a leader in the formative DBDM process you are not removed from this step. First, you need to work with the teaching faculty so that they understand that this is different from a traditional lesson plan–delivery approach. Part of the way you do this is by conducting learning walks to ensure the formative assessment process is being implemented with fidelity. We discuss more about this in Chapter 7, which is on assessment. This is not a "gotcha" process—you are engaged in formative assessment leadership and formatively working with the instructional staff to better integrate the principles discussed in this book into practice. Up to this point, you have led the initial data identification and evaluation steps, you have worked with teachers to plan, and now you are observing and supporting the Apply step. Although teachers are implementing the plans they developed, you need to actively observe and provide your own feedback to teachers to help support the instructional process. The cycle integrates all stakeholders of the instructional process—the students (as you will read more about in this section), the teachers, and the building leaders.

We have found a collegial approach to instructional supervision works best when providing teachers with feedback, particularly in the area of formative assessment. Because an emphasis on this practice is new to novice and veteran teachers alike, it is important for the observation model in your school to be one that encourages dialogue between teachers and administrators. We find too many administrators who forget that the purpose of teacher observation is to provide teachers with meaningful feedback through a process that enables faculty to be active participants in an effort to improve practice and ultimately enhance student achievement. In schools where a monologue occurs during the postobservation conference, the teacher observation process is viewed through a compliance lens, and feedback does not result in teacher growth. In schools in which administrators engage teachers in meaningful conversations about their practice throughout the observation cycle, job-embedded professional learning exists and the dialogue are often rich. Following are several strategies we have seen used by successful building administrators:

- Pre-observation conferences—Although this strategy requires a significant time investment on the part of the administrator, much is gained from the conversations that take place during these meetings. Regarding the topic of formative assessment, some administrators we work with hold these conferences with select teachers who are in need of more guidance than their peers are. These administrators wear a "coaching" hat during these meetings and strategically plan questions to engage teachers in a dialogue that results in a teacher having mapped out a plan for how formative assessment will be used during the lesson to be observed. By having an in depth understanding up front about which formative assessment strategies will be used, we have found both the observer and the teacher to be more reflective during the postobservation conference.

- Round-table PD sessions—One administrator we worked with spent time identifying best practices in the area of formative assessment within the building. A group of five to seven teachers was then asked to present these strategies during a faculty PD session. Rather than each teacher coming before the entire staff, the teachers divided into groups and spent approximately 10 minutes rotating through each station to learn about the various strategies. Following the PD, teachers were asked to select two new strategies to implement. Next, teachers invited an administrator to observe a lesson in which the strategies were incorporated into a lesson.

- Instructional rounds—Similar to the strategy used by medical students during medical school, some schools we have worked with use this strategy to enable groups of teachers to observe various formative assessment strategies in select classrooms or schoolwide. Immediately afterward, a debriefing meeting is held that results in meaningful dialogue. The focus of the conversation is on what was observed or not and not about specific classrooms.

Embedded into the lesson plans developed in the Plan step of the cycle must be a number of different formative assessments. These assessment tools and strategies enable teachers to carry out the collaboratively designed lessons plans and to utilize a number of formative assessment practices designed to engage students in the learning process in deep, substantive ways. In this step of the FAL cycle and in the Assess step, we share several useful formative assessment strategies that can be integrated into the instructional plan. The tools and strategies we share provide a taste of the myriad possibilities available to teachers for use in their own instruction. We encourage you to engage in a process that helps teachers explore different tools and strategies that work for their own classroom context.

As we have stated previously in this book, we continue to advocate for the intentional incorporation of students into the instructional process. This is critical. Students should not be passive observers of instruction and simply "receive" the lesson—students need to be aware of the learning intentions, to develop their own learning goals, and to iteratively assess their own learning progress throughout the instructional process. As you conduct your learning walks as a part of this process to ensure fidelity of implementation, you should "look for" student engagement and active involvement during your observations. The next time you are visiting or observing in a classroom, we encourage you to ask one or more students in the room the following question: "What are you learning today?" Too many times we have asked this question and had a student respond, "My teacher would like for me to finish this worksheet by the time class ends" or "I have to write this paper." In schools in which students are actively engaged in learning and the instructional process, you will frequently hear them restate the lesson learning intention in their own words when they are asked this question. In these classrooms, students also have a clear understanding of the success criteria and the manner in which the teacher will be assessing their understanding of the learning intention.

The learning intention provides clearer learning objectives for the teacher and can certainly be used to help bring clarity to the objectives for students and our model advocates extending this approach directly to students. The unpacking process is effective to clarify goals, and we know that learners who have clearer understandings of the learning intentions perform better. As teachers apply the carefully constructed lessons, student voice and participation need to be a part of the lesson.

In addition, self-monitoring opportunities and formative feedback from teachers have also been shown to improve student performance. The "I can" statements embedded in the model provide an excellent starting point for bringing formative assessment strategies to the student level, giving students a simple, yet effective way of self-monitoring their progress toward the goal.

An important part of the Apply step is built in opportunities for teachers and instructional leaders to reflect on observed changes in student interactions in the classroom and potential changes in engagement with the content, their classmates, and the teacher. Although test scores can reveal important information about student progress, they do not help educators recognize changes/improvement in the affective domains of learning. The next step of the cycle focuses more on formal means of assessing student progress, as well as on the use of formative assessment tools. During the Apply step, teachers should pay careful attention to what they are learning from the formative assessment tools integrated into the lesson. As teachers become more skilled—and more comfortable—with the use of formative assessment tools *while* teaching, they can make real-time changes to the instructional design of the lesson to better meet students' learning needs.

The affective domains of learning are most responsible for helping to produce the test score changes you hope to see. A simple reflective log utilized in the model is critical because in it, one gathers important feedback that informs consecutive iterations of the cycle building on lessons learned, promoting an intensifying development of internal capacity to sustain growth in teacher quality and student learning. We suggest you work with teachers to codesign a formative assessment monitoring log to take real-time measures of how students are doing in class. We do not advocate you make this a formal process that transitions into required log submissions by teachers using complicated templates that teachers "must" complete. This will work in opposition to your systemic change efforts to fully integrate formative assessment processes into your school's instructional culture. Draconian compliance activities will usually meet resistance that can undermine the success of your implementation efforts. The logs should be personalized and be developed by each teacher to match that person's instructional style, students, grade level, and content.

Feedback

Providing students feedback is an essential component of this step in the cycle. Remember what we discussed earlier in this book: "Formative assessment provides critical feedback to students while still working toward a learning goal." During this step of the process, teachers need to help students process their learning in the class with a focus on the following:

- **Goal setting** (Where am I going?)
- **Self-assessment** (How am I doing compared to my goal?)
- **Self-monitoring** (How am I progressing toward the goal?)

Without feedback, students are not able to accurately gauge their progress, make their own adjustments in their learning, and be self-regulated learners. Feedback allows students to understand how they are doing set against their learning goals and enables students to be active agents in their own learning. The use of feedback has been found to increase student effort in the learning process, increase student motivation, and increase student engagement in class (Deci, Koestner, & Ryan, 1999). In Hattie's (2013) meta-analysis in *Visible Learning* feedback was found to have a .73 effect size and to have a dramatic impact on student learning.

We have learned in our work that forward feedback (forward feedback provides information students can use to adjust their performance as they work toward a learning goal) is sometimes difficult for teachers to incorporate into their instructional approach if they were not trained in that manner. This transition in thinking and instructional application *is* possible—your role as a leader of the formative assessment process necessitates your active involvement in helping teachers with this transition. In this book, we are focusing on your work with teachers in the building and on you leading this process, rather than you working directly with students. However, we hope by now you are able to see the direct links among the PD process, and activities with building faculty, and the manner in which teachers can and should use many of the same processes and activities with their own students in their classrooms. Your PD with teachers on feedback should model principles of good instruction and the use of formative assessments.

7 Assess

The next step of the model provides the vital link to all the preceding steps by gathering empirical evidence of the impact of the evaluation of previous data, the identification of targeted areas of focus, and the associated planning and application of instructional and assessment strategies. It is during this step that teachers and instructional leaders are able to chart a course of action, ascertain which aspects of their planning and implementation were effective, which showed promise, and which seemed to miss the mark. Here, the data team members also collaboratively look at their reflective logs, data, and other evidence of student performance, and build the next iteration from a strengthened platform of success.

One of the challenges for educational leaders regarding this step of the model is that many teachers frequently consider assessment to be solely a means for measurement and evaluation rather than a cycle that also serves academic learning. Fisher and Frey (2007) shared the analogy of coaching to emphasize this principle, which is well established in athletics and the arts. For example, every effective coach understands that success in the game (i.e., summative assessment) begins in practice and that coaching involves similar repeated cycles of ongoing assessment, feedback, and instruction.

Moss and Brookhart (2009) used the metaphor of a windmill to visualize the formative assessment process and its effects. Just as a windmill can harness the power of moving air to generate energy, the process of formative assessment can help students to harness the workings of their own minds to *generate* motivation to learn. *Propelled* by the cycle of formative assessment, students' use of learning intentions, the establishment and the use of success criteria and the monitoring of students' own learning progress help learners develop into more confident and competent students as they become *energized* about learning and become considerably more able to regulate their own effort and actions during the learning process. When a windmill picks up speed, its individual blades disappear. When carried out correctly, the same can be said for the steps to the formative assessment process. It is important for educational leaders to understand this process and to be able to effectively communicate to teachers that ongoing assessment and adjustment are integral to improving student performance.

Formative Assessment Strategies

Although formative and summative assessment both play a role in the process of collecting, synthesizing, and interpreting information in the classroom for assisting the teacher in decision making, the focus of this book is on the formative assessment process. Because the background knowledge that students bring into the learning setting often has an impact on how they grasp content and respond to various learning opportunities, formative assessment becomes an important step in the process of teaching and learning that is often overlooked. In our experience, we have found many educational leaders make assumptions regarding teachers' knowledge of the characteristics of formative assessment, relying too heavily on undergraduate training and/or previous teaching experience in another school or district. Unfortunately, many teachers are not well versed in the differences between formative and summative assessment. In an effort to address misconceptions, and to provide quality professional learning opportunities, some school systems are beginning to place greater emphasis on this training during the new-teacher induction process, as well as other staff development venues.

During these learning opportunities for staff, training will often address the importance of providing a range of methods of assessment. In our experience, particularly in this era of accountability, we have found there to be an overreliance on one or two methods of assessment (i.e., multiple-choice and short-answer items). Compounding this fact is an overemphasis on the measurement of select skills viewed as heavily weighted items on end-of-year state assessments, and an environment is created that does not lend itself to adequately checking for student understanding during the learning process. In an effort to ensure tighter alignment between the written, taught, and tested curriculum, Wiggins and McTighe (1998) encourage us to think more like assessors. By asking questions such as "What would be sufficient and revealing evidence of understanding?" and "How will I be able to distinguish between those who really understand and those who don't (though they may seem to)?" will help teachers to avoid the overreliance on multiple-choice and short-answer assessments.

Earlier in the book we discussed the importance of unpacking standards in an effort to gain a clearer picture of the learning intentions. This step, as you will see, also plays a key role in providing a blueprint for assessing understanding and aiding teachers as they address the previously noted questions. Whether one is unpacking the Common Core or a state's standards, the big ideas, learning intentions, and success criteria for the standards contain the verbs that suggest the kinds of assessments needed to determine whether students are able to demonstrate understanding of the curriculum. Let us look at an example using the following standard: *The student will identify and describe the characteristics of prime and composite numbers.* In this example, in order to examine what would be sufficient and revealing evidence of understanding, it is essential that you pay close attention to the verbs. Although it would be relatively easy to search a canned question bank for multiple-choice questions to *identify* prime and composite numbers, it would be more difficult perhaps to locate questions in this question bank to address the verb *describe.* Not only is it critical for teachers to have a clear understanding of the essential knowledge associated with this standard; it is just as important for them to be strategic in their design approach to formative assessment. In this scenario, a teacher could use a variety of strategies to check for students' understanding of the second part of this standard. For example, the teacher could use a quick check to ask students to create two arrays to show whether a number is a prime or a composite or a think-pair-share activity in which students (a) listed by themselves the characteristics between the two types of numbers, (b) compared lists with a peer and discussed the characteristics of the numbers, and (c) created a final list to share with another pair of students.

Teachers can incorporate a host of activities to check for understanding and to help students self-monitor their progress. Often these activities are broken into two categories: (a) pre-assessment and (b) ongoing assessment. In addition, by varying the type of assessments used in either of these categories over the course of a week, it helps to paint a more accurate picture of what students understand.

Pre-Assessment

In order to plan appropriate and targeted learning experiences for students, an important factor is taking into account what the student already knows (Tomlinson & Moon, 2013). The teacher who incorporates pre-assessment in an effective manner, and on a regular basis, makes the statement that he or she has no intention of moving forward in the learning process until he or she has a clear understanding of the background knowledge the varied learners will bring to the content. Another important factor, and a point we have already discussed in detail, is the need for teachers to have a clear understanding about what students should know, understand, and be able to do as a result of the unit of study prior to creating any assessment. In addition, although it is not the intent of a pre-assessment to yield feedback surrounding each essential knowledge item in a unit of study, it is important to be able to ascertain students' background knowledge of the learning intentions and select skills that will be addressed during the unit.

Pre-assessment strategies can be informal or formal measures. Examples of informal measures do not typically involve gathering information for every student. These strategies, which may include KWL (What I Know, What I Want to Know, What I Learned) charts, thumbs-up/thumbs-down, student self-reporting, response cards, teacher observation, and personal-response computer systems, usually involve the teacher *taking a pulse* of students' knowledge, understanding, or skill. Examples of formal strategies for pre-assessment of student readiness, on the other hand, are for gathering data at the individual student level. Examples include journal entries/writing prompts, paper/pencil pretests, Frayer diagrams, student self-rating, show and tell, and systematic observations/interviews. The primary difference between informal and formal pre-assessment strategies is the manner in which instructional time is affected and the level at which information is obtained (Tomlinson & Moon, 2013). You will find that many of the informal and formal pre-assessment strategies are also appropriate for ongoing assessment. (See Figure 7.1 for descriptions of some informal and formal assessment strategies.)

Ongoing Assessment

It is also important for students to *know where they are* as a unit of study evolves. Figure 7.2 lists and describes some strategies that are frequently used

KWL Chart/Table—The letters *KWL* are an acronym for what students, in the course of a lesson, already **K**now, **W**ant to know, and ultimately **L**earn. A KWL table is a graphical organizer that is typically divided into three columns titled "Know," "Want," and "Learned." Prior to moving into a new topic of study, the teacher leads a discussion with the whole class on a topic, and student contributions are captured using this chart. As students' thoughts are captured on the chart, the teacher is able to create a general picture of overall student familiarity with the topic.
Thumbs-Up/Thumbs-Down or Signal Cards—Colored cards are frequently used with this strategy to check for understanding (i.e., green = "I have it," yellow = "I'm not sure; maybe," and blue = "I am confused and have questions"). As students hold up their cards in response to questions, the teacher is provided feedback by quickly checking the proportion of the students with the correct response. This strategy can also be used with hand signals (i.e., thumbs-up = "I have it," waving hand = "I'm not sure; maybe," thumbs-down = "I am confused and have questions").
Watch, Look, Listen—As teachers work with students throughout the day, simply observing the actions, behaviors, and words of students can yield valuable data which can inform planning for upcoming units of study. While many teachers are already having these conversations, the key is to be purposeful as to what information can be gleaned from these observations to use for instructional purposes. Some teachers will use a student roll sheet with this strategy to capture anecdotal notes that will be referenced during planning.
Individual Interviews or Observations—The teacher conducts individual conversations with students or observes them as they work or present work to check students' level of understanding. Teachers will often create checklists or guides to facilitate the capture of data with this strategy.
Ticket to Enter/Entry Card—Teacher asks a question the day prior to students moving on to a new unit/topic of study. Students are handed this question on a card prior to leaving the class with an expectation of responding on the card that evening. As students enter the class the next day, the teacher collects the cards and reviews the students' responses to gain a better understanding of students' background knowledge.
Show and Tell—Teacher asks a question, and the students both illustrate (*show*) and explain (*tell*) aloud and/or in writing what they know about the topic. Some teachers will use this strategy along with a think-pair-share activity.

Figure 7.1 Informal and Formal Assessment Strategies

for ongoing assessment. The goal of each of these strategies is to foster an understanding as opposed to simply evaluating. Results from these types of ongoing assessments inform students and teachers about both what skills students currently grasp and how to move forward with future teaching and learning.

It should be noted that the sample strategies listed in Figure 7.2 are by no means an exhaustive checklist. In fact, in many schools we have worked

Entry Cards—Students respond to a question that was shared at the end of the previous class or is posted for students upon entering the class. For ongoing assessment purposes, entry cards often relate to homework or to an important component of the previous day's lesson.
Exit Cards—Students respond to one or more questions posed by the teacher that are related to the day's lesson. Students' responses can be captured using index cards, scrap paper, or sticky notes and are collected prior to students leaving the room or change subjects within the room.
Quick Write—Students write for 2 to 3 minutes about what they heard during a lesson or an explanation, what they read, or what they learned. This could also be a response to an open-ended question from the teacher.
3–2–1—Students write three ideas, concepts, or issues presented, followed by two examples or uses of each idea/concept, followed by one unresolved question or item that presents confusion. The strategy can also be used with an arrangement of 1–2–3 and with a wide variety of prompts.
12-Word Summary—Students, in 12 words or less, will summarize the significant aspects of a particular piece of instruction or reading.
Circular Check—Working in groups, students are given a problem with a definitive answer. The first student in the group completes the first step without assistance from others in the groups and passes the problem on to the next student. The second student corrects any mistakes and completes the next step, again without input from others. These steps are repeated until the group has the correct answer. (This strategy works well in science and mathematics classrooms.)

Figure 7.2 Ongoing Assessment Strategies

with that are experiencing success with ongoing assessment strategies, teachers are frequently designing their own strategies based on the needs of their students, the particular content within a given grade level/department, and the contexts of their classrooms. Earlier we stated that many pre-assessment strategies can also be used for ongoing assessment, and the same can be said for ongoing assessment strategies and nearly all student work. It is important to remember the format is not as important as the intent of the assessment and as how teachers and students will use the results to inform learning are. As administrators continue their conversations with teachers, this point cannot be overstated.

Another point we would like to emphasize is the power of collaboration as it relates to ongoing assessment. In our experience, collective responsibility for student achievement helps to foster a culture of collaboration in schools. Similar to the lesson study model mentioned earlier in the book, when teachers approach assessment in a collaborative manner, students benefit from the power realized from this collective effort. In this scenario, teachers and administrators engage in meaningful conversations and work that result in a strategic approach to monitoring student progress and providing targeted instruction.

This work frequently begins with the creation of a common formative assessment (CFA). A CFA, which is an assessment or set of assessment items created collaboratively by a team of teachers responsible for the same grade or course, can be utilized for a variety of reasons. Following are several of the more frequent uses for this assessment strategy:

1. Used as a pretest to provide teachers with an overview of background knowledge of select skills that will assist to plan for instruction

2. Used at select points of time during a given unit of instruction as an assessment *for* learning

3. Used by teachers to drive intervention and/or remediation planning efforts

The word *common* implies that teachers are coming around the table to collaboratively construct these assessments. Discussion often occurs during these meetings about the types of items that will be included on the CFAs, when they will be administered, and the performance bands students will fall into once administered. The word *common* also implies teachers will come together following the administration of these assessments to collaboratively examine the results in an effort to determine next steps based on what the data showed. The discussion that emerges during these meetings is rich and frequently results in teachers refining their practices. For example, the dialogue provides teachers with a chance to discuss strategies used in lessons. Based on the results of the CFA, it could be the students in one teacher's classroom significantly outperformed students in the other teachers' classes on select skills. The collaborative manner in which the results are analyzed provides teachers with an opportunity to share specific strategies used during a given lesson that translated into positive student achievement results.

Modeling the Formative Assessment Process for Teachers

The formative assessment process relies on evidence to guide teaching and learning. When building administrators engage in ongoing, meaningful conversations with teachers through a collegial supervision model, they model the formative assessment process. Research supports the work of building administrators engaging in periodic, short, focused, individual conversations with a teacher (DiPaola & Hoy, 2014; Hall & Hord, 2000).

As states continue to apply for waivers from the U.S. Department of Education to move away from the sanctions associated with the No Child Left Behind Act, we are beginning to see a trend in districts and schools as they move from a more summative model of teacher observation and evaluation to one that is more formative in nature. In many instances, the waivers that have been granted across the country have required states to revamp their teacher evaluation process. As a result, it has become an opportune time for districts to reexamine their approach to teacher observation and the manner in which teachers receive feedback through this process.

In some of the schools we have been working with, formative data collection tools are being used with teachers to improve various facets of teaching. For example, the website onlineobservationtools.com contains a number of formative observation tools that can be used to support the teacher observation process. These tools would be ideal to use during the learning walks we discussed in the previous chapter. One of the tools on this website focuses on providing teachers feedback regarding the levels of questioning during a given lesson, whereas another provides feedback regarding student engagement. In both these instances, the observer sets out to capture and provide specific feedback to teachers via data collected through using the formative observation tool and the conference held with the teacher shortly following the observation. Data collection tools such as these help observers to capture objective data and are viewed by teachers as being nonthreatening in nature. The same cannot be said for many of the standard observation protocols being used by most school districts that address a number of different standards and often contain ratings associated with each standard. Similar to students receiving nongraded feedback through the formative observation process, teachers are more receptive to feedback that does not have a rating of "needs improvement" attached. In addition, administrators who have adopted this approach to teacher observation indicate that it has changed the postobservation conference from one of monologue to one of dialogue. It is important for students to become active agents in their learning, and the same can be said for teachers.

8 | Refine

The last step is closely tied to the assessment of impact but looks to future implementations and gathers lessons learned from all stakeholders and at all steps of the model. This feedback capitalizes on success and mitigates weaknesses by only promoting what was effective to subsequent iterations of the process. During this step, you catalogue lessons learned, creating a sort of locally produced and contextually relevant "What Works Clearinghouse" of effective practices. Cataloging effective practices links changes in student learning with instruction and builds internal capacity and professional confidence and trust in team members. We would argue this will increase motivation, professional respect, and buy-in to the model and, in turn, will stabilize the teacher workforce.

During the cycle, you and your data teams gathered evidence about the impact of the strategies applied and sought to determine which aspects of your planning and implementation were most effective. You explored which components of the plan demonstrated promise and which may have been ineffective. You also utilized worksheets in the book and/or found other materials to support your efforts. These represent a host of important insights and ideas that you will want to have at your disposal during the Refine step. Given this wealth of information you will now narrow your focus on the most effective practices, expand those clear successes, refine and strengthen those that demonstrated promise, and, when necessary, eliminate less effective practices.

There is one important caveat about eliminating less effective practices we want to discuss. A particular strategy may be ineffective for a variety of reasons. Before you make the decision to eliminate a strategy, carefully review how it was implemented. Determine if there were implementation weaknesses that explain the poor outcomes. This is particularly important if you are utilizing new instructional or assessment or practices outside of teachers' comfort zones. Although a fuller discussion of how one would evaluate the implementation of a strategy is beyond the scope of this book, we want to emphasize the need to encourage all stakeholders in the formative DBDM cycle to be cautious when making the decision to eliminate a strategy. You may discover that there were overlooked or misinterpreted features of the strategy, in which case you can invite teachers and others to refine their implementation with this feedback.

The Process of Refining

The first task is to gather the lessons learned by compiling the various worksheets and other materials you have developed and worked on thus far. Similar to the Data Wall discussed in the Identify section of the book, here you can utilize what we call the Refine Wall. With this adaptation of the data wall, your team will collaboratively identify strategies and other improvement efforts to focus on in the next iteration of the cycle.

In addition to identifying areas to refine and strengthen, you should also assess if there are common implementation challenges across strategies. In many cases there will be a common set of oversights, mistakes, misinterpretations, or other factors that limited the effectiveness of a strategy. Identifying these can help teachers pinpoint more specific refinements. This can be a powerful tool; once identified, those common implementation challenges can also provide insights and improvements well beyond the areas focused on during a particular iteration of the formative DBDM cycle.

The Refine Wall

As you have discovered, formative DBDM can be a space intensive effort with data walls and giant sticky notes spread out around the walls. This will continue to be the case during the final step of the cycle. (We suggest investing in large chart paper that can be used and moved throughout your formative DBDM process.) Being able to get up and walk around the room to explore what has been most effective and what areas can be refined and strengthened can be a very motivating experience for educators. Like many other parts of this cycle, the teachers themselves are driving growth and improvement in active and deliberate ways that support a number of principles of adult learning.

Both school leaders and teachers bring the strategies and other improvement efforts assessed in the previous step of the cycle. These are posted around your room to create the "Refine Wall." Participants then take a "gallery walk" and review what the group has learned about the strategies. For example you can ask questions such as "What strategies are working?" "What strategies hold promise?" and "What are we skeptical of continuing to use in our classrooms?"

Participants carefully review the data posted on the wall related to each individual strategy. During this process, each member needs to have a stack of sticky notes to use for commenting. For each strategy or improvement effort, participants will post one of the following three comments: Expand, Refine, or Considering Eliminating. On a different color sticky, participants will identify the possible areas for expanding, suggestions for refinements, and/or rationales for eliminating the strategy/improvement effort.

Next, participants will take a second gallery walk to review the categories and their associated next steps, as well as to identify common implementation challenges. Participants will post these themes on a third color sticky note. Next, the facilitator will post three large sticky notes (e.g., 22" × 33") labeled "Expand," "Refine," and "Eliminate" and will prompt a discussion about which strategies go into each category. Have a recorder capture this conversation, because this is valuable data point that can inform you about the current state of your school staff's formative DBDM understanding. You will also want to include in the conversation a discussion the common implementation challenges. Last, the facilitator will prompt a discussion about next steps and a "game plan" for where to reenter the cycle. The note taker will capture the plan and provide this to the group after the meeting.

As discussed earlier, it is important to document what happens in these Refine conversations. Capture these insights, commit them to writing (capture in an ongoing electronic tool your team develops), and find a way within your own school to institutionalize a "lessons learned" repository. This will promote the sustainability of your formative DBDM efforts. As you develop a catalogue of lessons learned and effective practices, you will be able to come back to this tool as use data to inform instructional decisions.

This catalogue can be developed in any number of ways. You need to find the one that works best within your school's technology structure. You may have a learning management system (such as BlackBoard, Moodle, etc.), an electronic server, or other technology where you can house these materials. Develop the best way of managing these lessons learned in your "What Works" catalogue so that you can refer back to them as a team and so that your teachers can refer to whenever they want to review the catalogue. This kind of locally produced and contextually relevant collection of effective practices linked to changes in student learning can be a powerful tool for promoting both individual and organizational capacity. Team leaders, data coaches, department chairs, or other instructional leaders could be responsible for developing and updating this catalogue at each iteration of the Refine step.

Even though Refine is the last step, the formative DBDM cycle should be seen as iterative. Having said this, however, instructional leaders should see the cycle as a flexible tool for guiding decision making and as not a strict process to be adhered to step by step. Once the refinements to the instructional strategies have been identified along with a game plan for next steps, it may not be necessary to begin at the top of the cycle with the full school wide data review and identification of key areas to work on in subsequent steps. Instead, teams might move past this aspect of the Identify step and begin looking at more targeted grade-level and/or content data. Similarly, depending on the circumstances, they might also move directly to the Plan step and quickly refine the game plan they already developed during their refining efforts and move into the Apply step (see Figure 8.1).

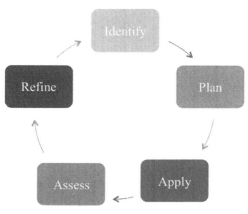

Figure 8.1 From Refine to Plan

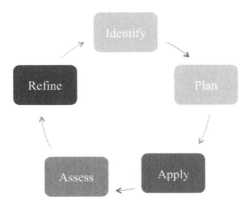

Figure 8.2 From Refine to Apply

In other circumstances, the game plan generated during the Refine Wall activity may be perfectly adequate, and the team could move directly to the Apply step (see Figure 8.2). It will be important for instructional leaders to use their professional discretion to guide these decisions.

Tools to Support the Cycle of Formative Data Based Decision Making

This section provides you and your team with worksheets, activities, and other tools that you can use as you lead the formative DBDM process. You should be prepared to tailor the tools to meet your own contextual setting. In some cases we also provide examples of how these tools may be used in the process. Each of these tools was referenced in different cycles of the formative DBDM process in the previous chapters of the book.

As we discussed earlier in the book, examples are beneficial to use in this process. At the end of this section, we have shared four scenarios you can use in your leadership team as you begin the formative DBDM process. These are good team-building activities to calibrate your understanding of the process and how to better work with the entire school as you lead the journey into implementing the formative DBDM cycle.

Worksheets

The Sense-Making Process

I. Initial formative DBDM Terminology Agreement—The Leadership Team

a. The Leadership Team should consist of, at a minimum, the principal and the assistant principals. It is recommended that individuals who are directly involved with the facilitation of the formative DBDM process be a part of the Leadership Team. Typically other members of the team include department and/or grade-level leaders, the special education coordinator, the assessment coordinator (if your school has one), and other key staff members instrumental in the organizational decision-making process.

b. Each member of the Leadership Team should list his or her top 20 data usage words. These are words that each person believes teachers in the school should be very familiar with and should be able to define. These words are the "high frequency" DBDM words used with staff.

c. The Leadership Team must agree on a uniform definition of each word. This process can provide valuable insight into the foundational under-pinnings of the use of data in schools. If there are discrepancies in the definitions, these should be explored and discussed and consensus about definitions should be reached prior to completing the process and surveying the school staff.

II. Surveying the Staff

a. Using individual charts for each staff member, ask the school staff to provide their own definitions of the top 20 data words chosen by the leadership team. If the Leadership Team is constrained for time, a reduced number of words can be used (10 or 15). It is recommended that this be conducted in a setting where all staff is present. If this is not possible, then a convenient process should be developed to survey the staff. A member of the Leadership Team should supervise this process.

b. The Leadership Team should carefully tabulate the results of the survey and discuss any discrepancies in term definitions at a separate Leadership Team meeting. Salient components/issues arising from the examination of the results should be identified and discussed.

c. The results of the tabulation and key issues should be shared with the school staff and discussed. This process can be conducted in a large- or small-group setting, depending on the individual needs of the school staff. This conversation is a pivotal component of the sense-making process and allows the group to come to a common understanding of the key DBDM terms. Additionally, other underlying potential barriers to DBDM success may arise that the Leadership Team can also address (either immediately or that can be tabled for research and address later on).

Deep Alignment: Linking Learning and Teaching

Alignment is **linking what is tested with what is taught.** This is important—if you do not teach what is measured or measure what you teach, the result will not be valid. However, alignment at this basic level does not do anything to improve teaching or learning; it merely assures you are measuring the same things that were taught. This type of alignment has a number of basic layers of standards, curriculum, and assessment that begin at the state level and end in the classroom.

Basic Model of Alignment

Layers of Standards, Curriculum, and Assessment Alignment

State Level	District Level
● Standards	● Standards
● Curriculum	● Assessments
○ Curriculum framework	○ State
○ Scope & sequence	○ Local district-level assessments
● State assessment	● Curriculum
○ Blueprints	○ Curriculum framework
	○ Scope & sequence
	○ Local pacing guides

Building Level	Classroom Level
● Standards	● Standards
● Assessments	● Assessments
○ State	○ State
○ Local district-level assessments	○ Local district-level assessments
○ Building-level assessments	○ Building-level assessments
○ Grades	○ Grades
● Curriculum	● Curriculum
○ Curriculum framework	○ Curriculum framework
○ Scope & sequence	○ Scope & sequence
○ Local pacing guides	○ Local pacing guides
	○ Lesson plans

This level of alignment addresses test validity, but not instruction and the types of learning experiences students are having in the classroom that will lead to deep, substantive learning. Hattie's (2009) meta-analysis found that about 60% of the questions teachers ask are at the recall level and that about 20% are at a procedural or behavioral level. This demonstrates the focus is often on what is called the "delivery of instruction." This is a primary focus on content and assessment, with less attention to the methods used to help student master the content.

Deep Alignment

The next layer of alignment must be deep pedagogical alignment—**the degree to which instructional methods outlined in lesson plans and then carried out in the classroom ensures that students will learn and retain information.** If the teaching methods rely primarily on direct expository instruction to passive learners, students are unlikely to retain information beyond the short-cycle classroom assessments. Here you see gaps between grade-level and district quarterly assessments as well as state assessments. In deep pedagogical alignment, you are addressing the iterative nature of instruction and learning.

To get at deep alignment for promoting real improvements in learning, you need to integrate pedagogy and learning in an interactive manner. Without this you cannot address the quality and/or the effectiveness of the curriculum, the instruction, and the students' learning behaviors. The following graphic includes what is often missing from alignment processes—the integration of instruction and learning into the alignment process.

Model of Deep Pedagogical Instructional Alignment

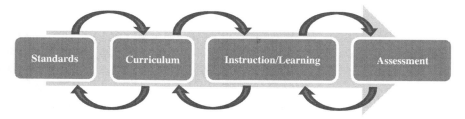

Aligning Pedagogy With the Level of Cognitive Complexity

Directions: Identify the standard you will be teaching in an upcoming unit and write it in the Standard column of the table that follows. Using Bloom's revised taxonomy, outlined after the table, identify the levels of cognitive complexity. This step helps educators think beyond discrete content and recognize the level of cognitive complexity associated with the standard. Last, utilizing the verbs associated with the different levels of the taxonomy, collaboratively brainstorm and identify possible instructional practices well suited to support the level of cognitive complexity identified.

Standard	Levels of Bloom's Taxonomy	Instructional practices that support the level of cognitive complexity
Example: All students should understand the relationships in the place-value system, in which each place is 10 times the value of the place to its right.	<ul><li>**Understanding**</li><li>Relationships imply **analyzing** as it requires determining how place value and multiplication are related.</li><li>Similarly there is an element of **evaluation** where the learners need to make judgments based on the concept of place value.</li></ul>	<ul><li>Hands-on learning</li><li>Problem-based learning</li><li>Demonstrations</li><li>Multiple means of representation, engagement and expression of understanding by students</li><li>Exemplars and models</li></ul>

Bloom's Revised Taxonomy

Remembering: Retrieving, recognizing, and recalling relevant knowledge from long-term memory

    Understanding: Constructing meaning from oral, written, and graphic messages through interpreting, exemplifying, classifying, summarizing, inferring, comparing, and explaining

Applying: Carrying out or using a procedure through executing, or implementing

Analyzing: Breaking material into constituent parts, determining how the parts relate to one another and to an overall structure or purpose through differentiating, organizing, and attributing

Evaluating: Making judgments based on criteria and standards through checking and critiquing

Creating: Putting elements together to form a coherent or functional whole; reorganizing elements into a new pattern or structure through generating, planning, or producing. (Anderson & Krathwohl, 2001, pp. 67–68)

Factors That Influence Learning Observation Tool

Directions: This tool, based on Hattie's (2013) book *Visible Learning*, is designed to help school leaders collect information about the degree to which these research-based factors are present across the school. Because this is a comprehensive list, it is unlikely you will observe all of these in a single day, so you may want to strategically focus on one to three areas at a time.

Use the Following Scale: 1, *Not Present;* **2,** *Surface Application;* **3,** *Present;* **4,** *Strongly Present*

Contributors to Student Learning	Impact on learning	Rating			
		1	2	3	4
1. The Student					
a. Self-reported grades	Very large				
b. Self-concept	Average				
c. Motivation	Average				
2. Home					
a. Parental involvement in learning	Average				
3. The School					
a. Principals and school leaders	Average				
b. Class size	Below average				
c. Ability grouping	Below average				
d. Within class grouping	Below average				
e. Retention	Negative				
f. Ability grouping for gifted students	Below average				
g. Acceleration	Large				
h. Enrichment	Average				

Contributors to Student Learning	Impact on learning	Rating			
		1	2	3	4
4. The Classroom					
a. Classroom management	Average				
i. Teacher's ability to identify and act quickly on potential problems	Very large				
ii. Teacher retaining emotional objectivity	Large				
iii. Effective disciplinary interventions	Large				
iv. Behavior targets	Large				
v. Tangible recognition of appropriate behavior	Large				
vi Direct and concrete consequences for misbehavior	Average				
vii. Teacher-student relationships	Large				
b. Group cohesion	Average				
c. Peer influences	Average				
5. The Teacher					
a. Teacher education	Below average				
b. Microteaching (analysis, reflective teaching, and post-discussions)	Large				
c. Quality of teaching	Average				
d. Teacher–student relationships	Large				
6. Teaching Strategies					
a. Setting goals	Average				
b. Concept mapping	Average				
c. Mastery learning	Average				
d. Worked examples	Average				
e. Feedback	Large				
f. Frequent testing/effects of testing	Below average				
g. Reciprocal teaching (summarizing, questioning, clarifying, and predicting)	Large				
h. Direct instruction	Average				
i. Problem-solving teaching	Average				
j. Computer-assisted instruction	Average				
k. Homework	Below average				

How Children Learn (Vosniadou, 2001) Classroom Observation Tool

Directions: This tool is designed to help school leaders collect information about the degree to which these research-based factors are present in classrooms. Because this is a comprehensive list, it is unlikely you will observe all of these in a single classroom visit, you may want to strategically focus on one to three areas per visit.

Use the Following Scale: 1, *Not Present;* **2,** *Surface Application;* **3,** *Present;* **4,** *Strongly Present*

Learning Environments: Active involvement	1	2	3	4
Avoid situations in which the students are passive learners				
Provide students with hands-on activities				
Encourage participation in classroom discussions and other collaborative activities				
Organize school visits to museums and technological parks				
Allow students to take some control over their own learning				
Taking control over one's learning means allowing students to make some decisions about what to learn and how				
Assist students in creating learning goals that are consistent with their interests and future aspirations				
Social participation				
Assign students to work in groups and assume different roles				
Create a classroom environment that includes group workspaces where resources are shared				
Modeling and coaching how to collaboratively learn				
Create circumstances for students to interact with each other, to express their opinions and to evaluate other students' arguments				
Link the school to the community at large				
Meaningful activities				
Situating learning activities in an authentic context				

Learning Environments: Active involvement	1	2	3	4
Cognitive Factors of Learning: Relating new information to prior knowledge				
Activate prior knowledge				
Investigate students' prior knowledge in detail so that false beliefs and misconceptions can be identified				
Teachers may need to go back to cover important prerequisite material or ask the students to do some preparatory work on their own.				
Help students see relationships between what they will be learning and what they already know				
Help students to grasp relationships and make connections				
Cognitive Factors of Learning: Being strategic				
Model the inquiry process				
Explicitly show students the learning behaviors they are interested in				
Provide scaffolding to ensure that students learn to use these strategies on their own				
Cognitive Factors of Learning: Engaging in self-regulation and being reflective. Teachers to provide student opportunities to do the following:				
Plan how to solve problems, design experiments, and read books				
Evaluate the statements, arguments, and solutions to problems of others, as well as of one's self				
Check their thinking and ask themselves questions about their understanding				
Develop realistic knowledge of themselves as learners; set their own learning goals				
Know what the most effective strategies to use are and when to use them				
Cognitive Factors of Learning: Restructuring prior knowledge				
Understand that students have prior beliefs and incomplete understandings that can conflict with what is being taught				
Create the circumstances where alternative beliefs and explanations can be externalized and expressed. Ignoring prior beliefs can lead to the formation of misconceptions.				
Provide students with observations and experiments that have the potential of showing to them that some of their beliefs can be wrong				
The importance of exemplars and models				
Depth over breadth				

Learning Environments: Active involvement	1	2	3	4
Cognitive Factors of Learning: Aiming toward understanding rather than memorization				
Ask students to explain a phenomenon or a concept in their own words				
Show students how to provide examples and illustrations				
Help students with domain specific problem solving and understanding their unique characteristics				
Help students see similarities and differences, compare and contrast, and generate analogies				
Teach students how to abstract general principles from specific cases and generalize from specific examples				
Cognitive Factors of Learning: Helping students learn to transfer				
Insist on mastery of subject matter. Without an adequate degree of understanding, transfer cannot take place.				
Help students see the transfer implications of the information they have learned				
Apply one subject matter area to other				
Show students how to abstract general principles from concrete examples				
Help students learn how to monitor their learning and how to seek and use feedback about their progress				
Teach for understanding rather than for memorization				
Cognitive Factors of Learning: Taking time to practice				
Increase instructional time				
Give students learning tasks that are consistent with what they already know				
Do not try to cover too many topics at once. Give students time to understand the new information.				
Engage in "deliberate practice" that includes active thinking and monitoring of their own learning				
Access to needed materials				
Support parents				

Learning Environments: Active involvement	1	2	3	4
Developmental and individual differences				
Learn how to assess children's knowledge, strategies and modes of learning adequately				
Use a wide range of materials, activities and learning tasks				
Help student identify their areas of strength and use them to mitigate weaknesses and how to use these insights to solve real-world problems				
Guide and challenge students' thinking and learning				
Ask children thought-provoking questions and test hypotheses				
Create connections to the real world				
Create circumstances for students to interact with people in the community				
Fostering Motivation				
Recognize student accomplishments				
Attribute student achievement to internal and not external factors				
Provide feedback to children about the strategies they use and instruction as to how to improve them				
Help learners set realistic goals				
Avoid ability level grouping. Ability grouping gives the message that ability is valued more than effort.				
Promote cooperation rather than competition. Research suggests that competitive arrangements that encourage students to work alone to achieve high grades and rewards tend to give the message that what is valued is ability and diminish intrinsic motivation.				
Provide novel and interesting tasks that challenge learners' curiosity and higher order thinking skills at the appropriate level of difficulty				

Notes:

Identifying Data to Make Decisions

This framework can help your team consider the types of data you want to use to make informed decisions about instruction. You can use the following framework with your leadership team and eventually with teacher groups, or for your own use as you process through how you are going to explore data to make decisions. The worksheet following the graphic is a tool you can use to evaluate the utility of the data source in your decision making process. We have found this worksheet provides a way to realistically evaluate the types of data you are using in your formative DBDM process in a rational way that promotes the safe psychological and innovative climate we advocate for in this process.

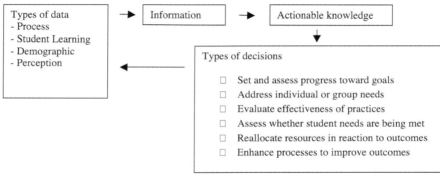

Types of data
- Process
- Student Learning
- Demographic
- Perception

→ Information → Actionable knowledge ↓

Types of decisions

☐ Set and assess progress toward goals
☐ Address individual or group needs
☐ Evaluate effectiveness of practices
☐ Assess whether student needs are being met
☐ Reallocate resources in reaction to outcomes
☐ Enhance processes to improve outcomes

Identify the level of data you are evaluating:

Level: ____ District ____ School ____ Grade Level ____ Subject Area
____ Classroom ____ Subgroups

Subject Area _____

Grade Level(s) _____

Type(s) of Data ____ Learning ____ Process ____ Demographics
____ Perception

Identify the intent of the use of this type of data:

What types of information can be obtained by the data?
What forms of actionable knowledge are sought?
What types of decisions can be made (informing decisions or action)?

Unpacking Standards to Create Learning Intentions

Cycle Steps

This template can be used in conjunction with the LEARNING INTENTIONS AND SUCCESS CRITERIA PLANNING FORM to assist teams with the process of "unpacking" standards.

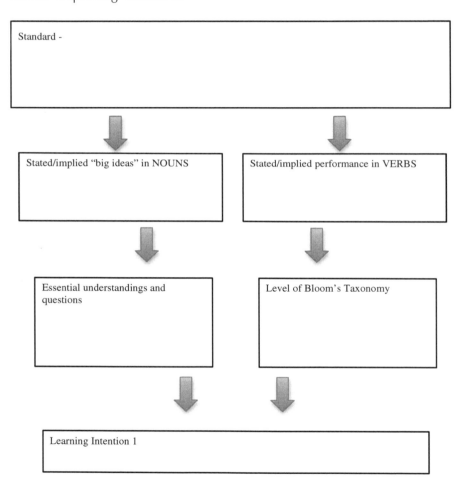

Standard -

Stated/implied "big ideas" in NOUNS

Stated/implied performance in VERBS

Essential understandings and questions

Level of Bloom's Taxonomy

Learning Intention 1

The Data Wall: Data That Sticks

The Data Wall has become standard practice in many schools. It is a good tool to visually sort through the clutter of data. Following is one approach instructional leaders can use (or adapt) to guide the process.

The idea of this data wall exercise is to pinpoint one area of focus for a teacher or administrator when trying to increase student achievement. This activity is interactive and visual. It walks participants through data clutter, weeds out the items they cannot change swiftly, and helps them focus on one or two actions to take in order to tackle a problem.

One of the key strategies for guiding this process is to keep asking "why" until you get to root causes and/or issues that you can target instructionally.

STEP 1: Administrator or teachers bring data, analyze for an issue or problem, and reach group consensus. Write the issue on a sticky note and put it on the top of the computer.

STEP 2: Groups look further at the data—when they find perceived underlying causes or reasons for what the data shows, they write those on stickies and put them on the computer. Stickies can be POSITIVE or NEGATIVE (e.g., lack of training vs. well-trained team).

STEP 3: Create a DATA WALL by transferring the stickies to a wall. Groups take a stretch break to look at the issue and reasons on the wall.

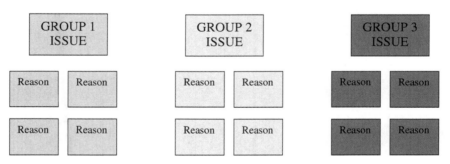

STEP 4: Categorize reasons by picking up the stickies and moving them onto BIG pieces of paper marked "Alignment," "Staffing/Scheduling," "Student Factors" (e.g., attendance, lack of accountability, behavior), "Curriculum," "Professional Development," and "Instruction."

STEP 5: Look for the one CATEGORY with the most stickies—this is where the focus should be with the exception of Student Behaviors. SB category may have many stickies, but SB is something that cannot be readily, swiftly changed.

FINAL STEP: Prioritize the STEP 5 category stickies.

The GROUP brainstorms action items leading to consensus on one or two actions to be taken to solve the problem.

Assessing the Conditions for Fostering the Development of the Whole Child

Blank and Berg (2006) provide a framework for the conditions needed to foster the development of the whole child. They emphasize that a narrow focus on outcomes on standardized tests can actually defeat the test's purposes by failing to recognize that lasting and transferable learning involves multiple and interconnected domains. We need to ask the question, What do our data tell us about the conditions needed to foster the development of the whole child?

6 conditions for fostering the development of the whole child	What do our data tell us about these 6 conditions? Where are our strengths and weaknesses and how might we utilize our strengths to mitigate our weaknesses?
1. The school has a core instructional program with qualified teachers, a challenging curriculum, and high standards and expectations for students.	
2. Students are motivated and engaged in learning—both in school and in community settings, during and after school.	
3. The basic physical, mental, and emotional health needs of young people and their families are recognized and addressed.	
4. There is mutual respect and effective collaboration among parents, families, and school staff.	
5. Community engagement, together with school efforts, promotes a school climate that is safe, supportive, and respectful and connects students to a broader learning community.	
6. Early childhood development is fostered through high-quality, comprehensive programs that nurture learning and development.*	

* May not be directly applicable to secondary schools.

Adapted from Blank, M., & Berg, A. (2006). *All together now: Sharing responsibility for the whole child.* Washington, DC: Association for Supervision and Curriculum Development.

Level of Understanding of Components of Effective Assessment

This table can be used by school administrators to determine teachers' level of comfort and understanding regarding some of the key components of effective assessment. The table can be distributed to individual teachers or can be completed in larger group settings by using "dot" labels and "sticky" notes.

Check a box to indicate your level of understanding for each of the following concepts:

- "3" means that you can provide a clear explanation of this concept as well as examples or other information to explain the term to others.

- "2" means that you are familiar with this concept but can provide only a limited explanation.

- "1" means that you currently cannot provide an explanation of this concept.

	3	2	1	Explanation (Use this column to record what you know about each item.)
"Unpacking standards" to create meaningful learning intentions				
Using Bloom's Taxonomy to address rigor within lessons and to construct assessments				
Using learning intentions to develop success criteria				

Lesson Plan/Assessment Preparation Form

This template is designed to assist teachers as they work in a collaborative manner to determine what learning experiences will be provided to students during a particular unit of study. Learning experiences outlined using this form should take into consideration the learning intentions and success criteria developed using the **Learning Intentions and Success Criteria Planning Form.** This form addresses the following key questions:

- Given the identified learning intentions, accompanying success criteria, and cognitive level, what learning experiences will be designed to best prepare students to demonstrate their understanding of these specific standards?

- What type of assessment strategies will enable the teacher to assess the appropriate level of rigor and to determine whether students are meeting/have met the targeted success criteria?

Step 1: List the learning intention, cognitive level, and success criteria.

- Learning Intention 1
- Cognitive Level
- Success Criteria

Step 2: Identify the student learning experiences that will be used to address this learning intention.

- Points to ponder when completing this step:
  - Will we incorporate whole group and differentiated activities?
  - Will we provide students with opportunities to set goals and self-assess during this unit of study?
  - Will we set aside time to explicitly share/teach the success criteria associated with this learning intention to students?
  - Will the learning experiences permit students to make connections between the activities and this learning intention/success criteria?

Step 3: List the assessment strategies that will be used to determine whether all students met the success criteria.

- Preassessment, entry cards
- Informal discussions, informal observations
- Work samples
- Matching, multiple choice, short answer
- Open-ended questions, exit cards
- Student self-assessment
- Essay
- Rubric (teacher graded or student self-assessed)
- Prompt
- Quiz
- Project
- Test

Learning Intentions and Success Criteria Planning Form

This template is designed to assist teachers as they work in a collaborative manner to ensure that a unit's essential learning intentions are clearly identified along with the success criteria students will be required to master.

> STEP 1: List the standards as outlined by your district's curriculum guide and/ or state curriculum framework document that will be taught during this unit of instruction.
>
> STEP 2: For each standard identified, work as a collaborative learning team to identify the essential learning intentions. (It is likely that the team will create more than one learning intention for each standard/skill.)
>
> STEP 3: As a team, discuss each of the learning intentions to determine/identify the appropriate cognitive level of demand. Using Bloom's Taxonomy (Remembering, Understanding, Applying, Analyzing, Evaluating, Creating), label the cognitive level for each learning intention.
>
> STEP 4: As a team, create success criteria for each learning intention. (It is recommended that these criteria are written in the form of "I can" statements. The success criteria can be used by individual teachers and collaborative learning teams to create both formative and summative assessments.)

Standard A:
Cognitive Level

Learning Intention	
Success Criteria	

_____

Standard A:
Cognitive Level

Learning Intention	
Success Criteria	

_____

Standard A:
Cognitive Level

Learning Intention	
Success Criteria	

_____

Standard B:
Cognitive Level

Learning Intention	
Success Criteria	

_____

Standard B:
Cognitive Level

Learning Intention	
Success Criteria	

_____

Standard B:
Cognitive Level

Learning Intention	
Success Criteria	

_____

A completed **Learning Intentions and Success Criteria Planning Form** can be used by teams to create a blueprint that can be referenced during the creation of assessments. This blueprint will help ensure that each learning intention is assessed at the appropriate level of rigor.

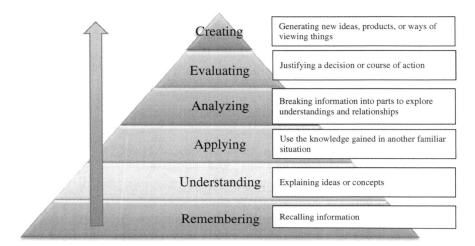

Learning Intentions and Success Criteria Planning Form (Example 1)

This is an example of how to use this worksheet.

This template is designed to assist teachers as they work in a collaborative manner to ensure that a unit's essential learning intentions are clearly identified along with the success criteria students will be required to master.

STEP 1: List the standards as outlined by your district's curriculum guide and/or state curriculum framework document that will be taught during this unit of instruction.

STEP 2: For each standard identified, work as a collaborative learning team to identify the essential learning intentions. (It is likely that the team will create more than one learning intention for each standard.)

STEP 3: As a team, discuss each of the learning intentions to determine/identify the appropriate cognitive level of demand. Using Bloom's Taxonomy (Remembering, Understanding, Applying, Analyzing , Evaluating, Creating), label the cognitive level for each learning intention.

STEP 4: As a team, create success criteria for each learning intention. (It is recommended that these criteria are written in the form of "I can" statements. The success criteria can be used by individual teachers and collaborative learning teams to create both formative and summative assessments.)

Standard A: *The student will recognize and describe a variety of patterns formed using numbers, tables, and pictures and extend the patterns, using same or different.*

Big Idea: *Recognize, describe, and extend geometric patterns*

Cognitive Level	
Remembering	Learning Intention 1—**Recognize the structure of a geometric pattern and how it grows or changes by identifying the core of the pattern.**
	Success Criteria 1—**I can name the rule of a growing pattern. I can name the rule of a repeating pattern.**
Understanding	Learning Intention 2—**Describe repeating and growing geometric patterns and understand that patterns can be translated from one representation to another.**
	Success Criteria 2—**I can write in my own words the rule of the growing pattern. I can write in my own words the rule of a repeating pattern.**
Applying	Learning Intention 3—**Extend geometric patterns using concrete objects or pictures.**
	Success Criteria 3—**I can tell or draw what figures come next in a repeating pattern using (a) concrete items and (b) pictures. I can tell or draw what figures come next in a repeating pattern using (a) concrete objects and (b) pictures.**

Learning Intentions and Success Criteria Planning Form (Example 2)

This is an example of how to use this worksheet.

This template is designed to assist teachers as they work in a collaborative manner to ensure that a unit's essential learning intentions are clearly identified along with the success criteria students will be required to master.

> **STEP 1: List the standards as outlined by your district's curriculum guide and/ or state curriculum framework document that will be taught during this unit of instruction.**
>
> **STEP 2: For each standard identified, work as a collaborative learning team to identify the essential learning intentions. (It is likely that the team will create more than one learning intention for each standard.)**
>
> **STEP 3: As a team, discuss each of the learning intentions to determine/identify the appropriate cognitive level of demand. Using Bloom's Taxonomy (Remembering, Understanding, Applying, Analyzing, Evaluating, Creating), label the cognitive level for each learning intention.**
>
> **STEP 4: As a team, create success criteria for each learning intention. (It is recommended that these criteria are written in the form of "I can" statements. The success criteria can be used by individual teachers and collaborative learning teams to create both formative and summative assessments.)**

Standard A: *The student will summarize supporting details from the text, summarize supporting details from nonfiction texts, determine the main idea of text, and summarize supporting key details.*

Big Idea: *Identify, compare, and contrast relationships between characters, events, and facts.*

Cognitive Level	
Understanding	Learning Intention 1—**Identify relationships between characters, events, and facts in non-fiction texts.**
	Success Criteria 1—**I can find information about important people, events, and facts in nonfiction texts.**
Analyzing	Learning Intention 2—**Compare and contrast relationships between characters, events, and facts.**
	Success Criteria 2—**I can explain how important people, events, and facts are similar or different.**
Evaluating	Learning Intention 3—**Evaluate comparing and contrasting relationships between characters, events, and facts.**
	Success Criteria 3—**I can discuss how the similarities and differences between important people, events, and facts impact the meaning of text.**

Planning for Success

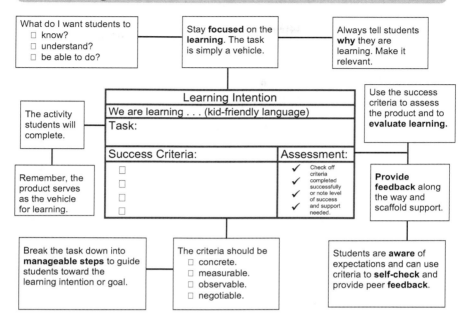

What do I want students to
- know?
- understand?
- be able to do?

Stay **focused** on the **learning**. The task is simply a vehicle.

Always tell students **why** they are learning. Make it relevant.

The activity students will complete.

Learning Intention
We are learning . . . (kid-friendly language)

Task:

Use the success criteria to assess the product and to **evaluate learning**.

Remember, the product serves as the vehicle for learning.

Success Criteria:
- ☐
- ☐
- ☐
- ☐

Assessment:
- ✓ Check off criteria completed
- ✓ successfully or note level of success
- ✓ and support needed.

Provide feedback along the way and scaffold support.

Break the task down into **manageable steps** to guide students toward the learning intention or goal.

The criteria should be
- ☐ concrete.
- ☐ measurable.
- ☐ observable.
- ☐ negotiable.

Students are **aware** of expectations and can use criteria to **self-check** and provide peer **feedback**.

Student Monitoring Log

Directions: Use the space below to record the Big Idea(s), Learning Intention(s), and Success Criteria. This log should be maintained by students and used to monitor progress as they work towards meeting or exceeding the success criteria during a unit of study.

Big Idea	Learning Intention	Success Criteria	
Concrete			☐
Representational			☐
Abstract			☐
Big Idea	**Learning Intention**	**Success Criteria**	
Concrete			☐
Representational			☐
Abstract			☐

7th Student Monitoring Log (Example)

Directions: Use the space below to record the Big Idea(s), Learning Intention(s), and Success Criteria. This log should be maintained by students and used to monitor progress as they work towards meeting or exceeding the success criteria during a unit of study.

Big Idea — Use roots, cognates, affixes, synonyms, and antonyms to expand vocabulary

	Learning Intention	Success Criteria	
Concrete	Use common Greek and Latin affixes and roots to predict the meaning of unfamiliar words.	I can use Greek and Latin prefixes, suffixes, and roots to figure out what a word means.	☐
Representational	Separate and recombine known word parts to predict the meaning of unfamiliar words.	I can separate and recombine known prefixes, suffixes, and roots to figure out the meaning of unknown words.	☐
Abstract	Use word structure to analyze and find relationships among words.	I can use word structures (prefixes, suffixes, roots) to find relationships between words.	☐

Big Idea — Describe the impact of word choice, imagery, and literary devices including figurative language.

	Learning Intention	Success Criteria	
Concrete	Recognize that authors make deliberate choices to create literary works.	I can recognize that authors make specific choices to craft their writing.	☐
Representational	Understand that language has an impact on readers.	I can understand the impact word choice and language has on the reader.	☐
Abstract	Analyze how figurative language enriches text with word images and figures of speech.	I can examine how figurative language makes texts better by using word images and figures of speech.	☐

8th Student Monitoring Log (Example)

Directions: Use the space below to record the Big Idea(s), Learning Intention(s), and Success Criteria. This log should be maintained by students and used to monitor progress as they work towards meeting or exceeding the success criteria during a unit of study.

Big Idea — **Make connections between any two representations given tables, graphs, words, or rules.**

	Learning Intention	**Success Criteria**	
Concrete	Graph in a coordinate plane ordered pairs that represent a relation.	I can use the vocabulary to recognize ordered pairs and graph them on a coordinate plane that shows a relation.	☐
Representational	Describe and represent relations and functions, using tables, graphs, words, and rules.	Given one representation, I can show the relation in another form different from the original one given.	☐
Abstract	Relate and compare different representations for the same relation.	I can share and explain different illustrations for the same relation.	☐

Big Idea — **Determine the domain and range of a given set of data.**

	Learning Intention	**Success Criteria**	
Concrete	Recognize and apply the following algebraic terms appropriately: *domain, range, independent variable*, and *dependent variable*.	I can use the vocabulary to recognize domain, range, independent variable, and dependent variable as needed.	☐
Representational	Determine the domain and range of a function as well as the independent and dependent variable of a relationship.	I can determine the domain and range of a function as well as the independent and dependent variable of a relationship.	☐

Addressing Barriers to Learning Intentions

Learning Intention	Assumptions of the strategies used to achieve the learning intention	Things the organization does (or fails to do) that work against the improvement learning intention?	Competing commitments— What are the behaviors, beliefs, biases, or assumptions that are incongruent with the learning intention?	Name the barrier to change

Glossary

Active agency Students taking active responsibility for their own learning supported by educator scaffolding.

Alignment: Deep (pedagogical alignment) Lesson plans, pacing guides, and other planning materials aligned with content and levels of cognitive rigor, cross-disciplinary opportunities to teach and/or reinforce, utilize formative feedback and other strategies that recognize that learning is complex, inter-related, and does not take place on a strict or predictable timeline.

Alignment: Surface The sequential alignment of discrete content and testing schedules.

Articulating theory from practice Structuring applied opportunities for educators to experience firsthand the underlying concepts or theories behind research-based strategies.

Assessment literacy A well-balanced set of skills and knowledge related to formative and summative assessment.

Big idea The product of an activity that deconstructs the underlying concept(s) for a given learning standard by identifying the verbs that indicate the types of assessments needed to determine whether students are able to demonstrate their understanding of the standard.

Clarify learning goals (goal setting) Helping students and teachers develop clear and in-depth understandings of learning goals or targets.

Climate of psychological safety Stakeholders in a school organization take risks, try out, and refine new ideas and strategies in a supportive environment.

Cycle of formative data based decision making A five-stage approach to data based decision making that involves identifying learning and instructional issues through data analysis, collaborative planning to address these issues, applying the plans, assessing the impact of these efforts, and refining the efforts based on iterative feedback.

Data based decision making A process of making purposeful decisions and systematically collecting, reviewing, and interpreting data, followed by empirically grounded actions.

Deconstruct Breaking down the learning and teaching goals or curriculum into their discrete components as a part of strategy for better understanding how these function in the aggregate.

Engagement The degree to which an individual is directly involved in learning or other activities.

Formative assessment Assessment information about performance or other efforts that individuals or groups use to adjust subsequent efforts.

Forward feedback Sharing information about student's performance or other efforts specifically designed to help move the student forward in learning.

Goals Can be used to describe both teaching and learning targets or desired outcomes; these help participants to be clearer about their purpose.

Goal displacement The tendency for organizations to lose sight of, or be deflected from, their stated goals.

Goal-setting Clarifying and then communicating teaching and/or learning intentions and purpose; essentially asking the question, "where am I going?"

"I can" statements Teachers' facilitating students' reviewing unpacked standards by outlining the specific competences the students will master during the lesson.

Instructional rounds A strategy for small groups of educators to visit classrooms, observe teaching and learning, and hold discussions about what was observed.

Intentional learner Learners who have clear learning targets, know what quality looks like, and seek out feedback to adjust their performance as they move toward the goal.

Learning intention The primary areas of content and/or instructional focus.

Lesson study model A collaborative approach to exploring various aspects of a lesson.

Metacognition Awareness of one's own thought processes.

Modeling Demonstrating the desired behaviors and actions for students to draw from as they work toward mastering various skills and knowledge.

Multiple measures of data Data representing school processes, demographics, perceptions, and student learning.

Observation cycle A leadership observation formative strategy that can include pre-observation conferences, classroom observations, instructional rounds and other approaches to gaining insights about instruction, providing feedback, and monitoring progress.

Pre-assessment An assessment prior to learning used to gain an understanding of where students are in relationships to a learning goal.

Problem statement Identify the central area or areas of concern that will give focus to data based decision making efforts.

Professional learning communities An approach to school improvement that places the responsibility of student success on the collective efforts of the school and where educators work in a culture of collaboration and professionalism.

Scaffolding Providing structure and support for learners to facilitate autonomy and self-regulation.

Self-assessment Students evaluating their own learning efforts in reference to their learning goals.

Self-monitoring Learners keeping track of their progress toward a learning goal.

Self-regulated learning Involves the learner taking direct and active control over his or her own learning through metacognition, goal setting, planning, assessing, self-monitoring, and assessing progress toward a learning goal.

Student error patterns Analysis of student performance data that identifies patterns of student misconceptions and errors, which can then be used to make iterative adjustments and improvements to instruction.

Success criteria Students are provided opportunities to develop clear understandings of what success will look like for a given unit of study, which help students to shift from general success goals to specific actionable goals.

Summative assessment Assessment of achievement at the end of a specific period, that is, after learning has occurred.

Teacher efficacy The degree to which teachers feel capable in their ability to perform in their professional roles.

Unpacking Deconstructing or breaking down the learning target into its basic elements to more fully understand the learning goal.

Data Scenarios

Scenario 1

The Background

A sixth-grade mathematics data team has developed an instructional plan based on a detailed analysis of previous test scores, along with the unpacking of the upcoming learning objectives. Through this effort they attempted to establish a more deeply aligned instructional approach that moves beyond surface alignment to an approach that has more carefully considered the appropriate level of cognitive rigor while fostering deep, pedagogical alignment. The group's analysis of the previous quarterly assessment, which covered standards in measurement, indicated patterns of errors in student conceptual understanding of measurement. These errors denoted students' basic misunderstandings of converting units of measure from length, area, weight/mass, and volume. Teachers readily recognized that these patterns of mistakes were similar to those made by students across all strands. Students struggled with core conceptual understandings of fractions, decimals, and percentages. With this knowledge as the background, the group moved on to unpacking the upcoming standards that covered a portion of the probability and statistics standards.

The group unpacked the standards identifying the learning intentions, the "I can" statements, and the level of cognitive rigor by assessing the verbs for their placement within Bloom's taxonomy, as well as learning intentions identifying those math concepts from the previous units of instruction and concepts students struggled with (and would likely present challenges to this next unit). With this done, the group set about designing instructional units that would specifically address the contextual issues they unearthed through their analysis and deliberations.

The Planning

The sixth-grade mathematics team, using the background they had developed, designed a three week unit which included the following elements: (1) pretesting on the standards, (2) dividing the students into leveled groups based on the pre-assessment, (3) intensive remediation for the lower performing students and problem-based learning activities to the more advanced students, and (4) a final applied project that would require the students to identify a topic, collect data, and report their findings using the skills developed during the unit.

The Application

The group's pretesting efforts revealed both in-class and within-group variation in performance, with some classes scoring at the remediation level and one scoring predominantly at the enrichment level. Teachers with the lower performing students felt frustrated that they had spent time developing problem-based plans but felt that they could not use them with their students. During the Apply step of the effort, many teachers became frustrated that their students were not responsive to what they felt were more fully developed units. Anecdotal evidence that suggested the pattern of errors identified in the early stage of the model were resilient to change and, even after focusing on those skills more intently, students continued to struggle. By the end of the unit, many of the lower performing students did not seem prepared for the applied project and turned in subpar assignments that missed many of the criteria laid out in the rubric. As the group prepared to test the students on the unit, a small majority of teachers were pessimistic that they would see any improvements in student performance.

Prompts for the Instructional Leader

1. What aspects of the process from identify to planning to application were not effectively thought through or implemented?

2. What support or interventions could the instructional leader have provided to help address these issues?

3. What feedback could the instructional leader provide as the group prepares to identify areas for improvement and refinements?

4. What aspects of the process were most successful, and why?

Scenario 2

The Background

Several years ago a new principal was assigned to an average-size elementary school in a metropolitan school district and was tasked with transforming the school to be "data driven." The principal had limited knowledge on how to use data to move her school forward. However, she found an abundance of data for many different areas such as home reading, accelerated reading, district-level assessments, attendance data, and so much more in notebooks kept by the previous administration. Her biggest challenge was deciding what was most important to make a difference for each student, and as such she struggled with the following question: "How can I make sense of this overwhelming information and use it to inform instruction?"

The Planning

To address this question, the principal began by examining the research on assessment and on DBDM and listened to her colleagues as they shared their experiences. She found considerable variation in practices of looking at the alignment of the curriculum and the instruction through the "eyes" of assessment in order to change results. To get stakeholder buy-in, she engaged the faculty in conversations designed to define what the practice of formative DBDM would look like, how teachers would be affected by it, how the students would be involved in the process, and, most important, what would the change process look like. She invited teachers to think about the variations and sent several teachers to visit other schools that would allow them to see the practices firsthand. During this search, the school's faculty had conversations with district leaders and university professors to examine other possible options within the continuum of assessments.

Through these conversations they heard old and new terms associated with data driven decision making, such as *common monthly assessments, Form A and Form B testing, formative assessments, assessment of learning, assessment for learning*, and many more. After this exploration and faculty involvement, the principal lead the school through an approach to DBDM that was not to prepare students for the next assessment but to prepare them for the next level of learning.

The Application

Ultimately the school constructed a system that supported the district's goals while involving students as part of the assessment process. The key difference between the new principal's school and many other learning environments was the role of teachers and students as consumer and users of assessment information. Teacher teams were tasked with looking at assessment information on an ongoing basis instead of once of month. The process included developing a clear understanding of information through shared conversations, feedback, and professional development activities. To collectively make sense of the practices and strategies, work was needed to build a culture of trust that spoke to accountability, transparency, and better decision making for improved student results. The principal discovered that it was not enough to present the strategies; the teams had to develop the type of trust that gave them the confidence to try out ideas. As the staff gradually moved along the assessment continuum, there was improvement with identifying gaps among the students, applying new strategies such as unpacking the standards, and quickly responding to customizing a plan of action at the teacher level. Trends became foreseeable as teachers continuously reviewed relevant information and responded to the data with instructional changes.

This new assessment cycle started to become an organic part of the instructional process that invited students to examine their own learning. The school shifted from heavily relying on multiple-choice assessments to including a mix of performance-based assessments that gave students the context for applying their learning while the teachers acted as observers provided feedback to students to help them improve their own learning. Since the implementation of the use of formative DBDM practices, the school continues to increase state-level results and shows a positive trend as students are becoming better learners and not just better test takers.

Prompts for the Instructional Leader

1. What aspects of the process from identify to planning to application were effectively or ineffectively thought through or implemented?

2. What additional supports or interventions could the principal or other instructional leaders have provided to help facilitate this change process?

3. What aspects of the process were most successful and why?

4. What obstacles might other school leaders face when attempting to model a similar change process?

5. What strategies would be effective in overcoming these challenges?

Scenario 3

The Background

The principal of a metropolitan middle school, whose results on the state standardized testing had been in decline for 5 years, initiated collaboration with an assessment specialist from a nearby university. To ensure the collaboration would meet the school's needs and be effective, the principal included a number of key stakeholders including an assistant principal, a curriculum specialist, and several teacher representatives in the planning efforts. The group met several times to identify needs and to settle on a course of action.

The Planning

During these planning meetings, the team reviewed both yearly and quarterly test scores and discussed the schools overall instructional and assessment climate. The team members were interested in identifying the appropriate starting point for increasing the effort's chances of success. All the school-level participants expressed concerns about tensions among the district push to increase test scores and their interest in addressing longer term instructional and learning issues. They felt pressured to produce short-term increases in student performance and felt that the only means of doing so was direct instructional of content rigorously aligned to the district's pacing guides. The feeling was that if the group were going to venture outside the evolving form of DBDM that identified lower performing students and put them in remedial groups, then clear and concrete strategies that teachers could put into action in their classrooms quickly and effectively would be needed. The group believed that such an approach would give teachers firsthand experiences with alternatives to the dominant model and would allow them to build a more effective data climate from their own growing expertise. These meetings resulted in agreement to pilot an approach to formative DBDM. The grade-level team was receptive and was provided training focused on three actionable formative assessment strategies that represented core conceptual understandings of formative assessment and provided a structure for teachers' to utilize these strategies in their classrooms. The teachers agreed to document the impact on student learning and to collaborate with colleagues to refine and strengthen their use over time.

The Application

The project was primarily implemented through an iterative process involving the teachers' learning about and utilization of new strategies and collecting data about effectiveness, while collaborating to understand and strengthen future use of the strategies. The team provided teachers with outside support and information they needed to enhance their professional expertise and all training was conducted during the normal school day on a monthly basis in the team leader's classroom. The first strategy introduced addressed the formative assessment principal of goal setting, utilizing the simple strategy of "unpacking" the learning objective and rewriting it in student friendly language. One of the teachers discussed how, out of the five sections of mathematics that he taught each day, between 15 and 20 students were failing math. As he described it, these students would not take notes, could not articulate what happened in class the previous day, and were generally passive in their orientations toward learning. As the group worked together, these students became known as the "Resistant 15" and were described as not completing any assignments, *"regardless of cajoling, threatening, warning . . ."* As a result of utilizing the unpacking strategy, this teacher articulated that the approach "caused an immediate transformation in some of the students" and that the *"Resistant 15 were dwindled down to roughly 9 or 10 students who remained Resistant."* He described how, because of using the unpacking strategy, some of the resistant students *"began to take ownership of their learning. Many students even began to refer back to their notes whenever there was a question or confusion regarding a certain topic."* Changes in learning were also observed by other teachers, and they developed a growing commitment not only to the concept of unpacking the learning objectives but also to the larger concept of extending goal setting to the students and the importance of active involvement in this process.

As the group went through each of the other strategies (defining quality work through student participation in rubric development and how to use data to provide forward feedback), the group became increasingly comfortable with the core ideas of formative assessment and how they could blend the use of various student performance data into their planning and instruction. One of the more notable lessons learned came from varying needs of the different content areas and how these influenced the application of the use of data and formative assessment practices. The group became increasingly comfortable and adapted the core principles to the specific needs of the subject area. There was evidence the teachers were taking increasing professional discretionary authority for their work.

What was important about this initial experience was the group noticed the teachers' participants had opportunities to utilize a relatively simple strategy in their classrooms and then had opportunities to actively participate in refining and strengthening the approach before implementing again. The group's process was facilitated by an inquiry-based approach to professional development that included engineered opportunities for the group to observe each other, the instructional specialist to make nonevaluative observations of the teachers, and discussing their experiences and observations with each other and with the university faculty involved in the project and administrators. Focus group interviews at the end of the year indicated that teachers felt that without the stakeholder planning and field-based approach to application of the formative assessment and DBDM topics, the effort would not have been as successful.

Prompts for the Instructional Leader

1. What aspects of the process from identify to planning to application were effectively or ineffectively thought through or implemented?

2. What additional supports or interventions could the principal or other instructional leaders have provided to help facilitate this change process?

3. What aspects of the process were most successful, and why?

4. What obstacles might other school leaders face when attempting to model a similar change process?

5. What strategies would be effective in overcoming these challenges?

Scenario 4

The Background

In a large suburban school district, the superintendent called a meeting of high school principals to announce a new initiative that would require schools to be "data driven." This initiative would begin over the summer and would provide training to principals and department chairs, who would in turn train the teachers and other personnel in their buildings. A book that was to be the district's "handbook" was handed out to the group to guide the educators to effectively implement these new practices. After the initial training, the principal at one of the high schools called a meeting of his teachers and set out the parameters of the new data driven initiative. The new initiative would require teachers be able to support *all* instructional decisions in data and preference to requests for new programs, money, or equipment would be tied to the degree to which the teachers could support their request in data. Teacher observation walk-through forms, lesson plan evaluations, and teacher evaluation protocols were modified to assess the use of data.

The Planning

The principals tasked department chairs with the primary responsibility of carrying out both the data driven training and the implementation of the new requirements. In the week prior to student starting the school year, department chairs ran in-house professional development workshops and disseminated articles and other resources about data driven decision making. Teachers were primarily passive in these training sessions, with some of them working on their lesson planning and other prep work. Before the students arrived, there was a negative atmosphere in the building around the term *data*. During the first 9 weeks, additional training was provided after which time all new policies regarding data went into effect.

The Application

All faculty meetings after the Implementation step of the initiative had a data item on the agenda. Various administrators, department chairs, and subject area specialists presented student performance data to the faculty in hand-outs and PowerPoint presentations. Similarly, departments established "data teams," which were tasked to give guidance to department. These teams were required to meet on a weekly basis to review benchmark data and to make recommendations to the faculty. Most of the data teams utilized this time to identify low- and high-performing students and to design remediation and enrichment lessons. No examples of data teams using benchmark scores to assess the level of rigor of the content, to examine patterns of student errors and misconceptions, or to question the instructional effectiveness of the approaches used to teacher the content were found.

School leaders who were responsible for teachers' supervision began to utilize the data criteria in their evaluations. Teachers began noticing that the "data driven" check boxes on the walk-through form were being checked off if there was any evidence of the use of data. Teachers shared this observation in informal discussions and began peppering their rooms with evidence of using data. Similarly, some school leaders privately admitted they really were not sure what they were looking for during the observations. In an end-of-year survey, teachers uniformly rated the initiative very low. Open-ended comments were particularly critical and demonstrated that most of the teachers felt the notion of being "data driven" was largely dogmatic district speak and was just another trend. As the teachers left for the summer, no mention was made of improvements or reforms to the initiative.

Prompts for the Instructional Leader

1. What aspects of the process from identify to planning to application were effectively or ineffectively thought through or implemented?

2. What additional supports or interventions could the principal or other instructional leaders have provided to help facilitate this change process?

3. What aspects of the process were most successful, and why?

4. What obstacles might other school leaders face when attempting to model a similar change process?

5. What strategies would be effective in overcoming these challenges?

References

American Psychological Association. (1993). *Learner-centered psychological principles: Guidelines for school redesign and reform.* Washington, DC: Author. Retrieved from ERIC database. (ED371994)

American Psychological Association. (1995). *Learner-centered psychological principles: A framework for school redesign and reform.* Washington, DC: Author. Retrieved from ERIC database. (ED411493)

Anderson, L. W., & Krathwohl, D. R. (Eds.). (2001). *A taxonomy for learning, teaching and assessing: A revision of Bloom's taxonomy of educational objectives: Complete edition.* New York, NY: Longman.

Bernhardt, V. (2004). *Data analysis for continuous school mprovement* (2nd. Ed). New York, NY: Routledge.

Bernhardt, V. (2013). *Data analysis for continuous school improvement.* New York, NY: Routledge.

Bernhardt, V. L. (2003). *Using data to improve student learning in elementary schools.* Larchmont, NY: Eye On Education.

Black, P., & Wiliam, D. (1998). Assessment and classroom learning. *Assessment in Education, 5*(1), 7–74.

Blank, M., & Berg, A. (2006). *All together now: Sharing responsibility for the whole child.* Washington, DC: Association for Supervision and Curriculum Development.

Blau, P. M., & Scott, W. R. (1962). *Formal organizations: A comparative approach.* San Francisco, CA: Chandler.

Bloom, B. S. (1968). Learning for mastery. *Evaluation Comment, 1*(2), 1–12.

Bloom, B. S., Hastings, J. T., Madaus, G. F., & Baldwin, T. S. (1971). *Handbook on formative and summative evaluation of student learning* (Vol. 923). New York, NY: McGraw-Hill.

Borko, H. (2004) Professional development and teacher learning: Mapping the terrain. *Educational Researcher, 33*(8), pp. 3–15

Bransford, J. D., Brown, A. L., & Cocking, R. R. (Eds.). (2000). *How people learn.* Washington, DC: National Academies Press.

Brookhart, S. M. (1991, Spring). Grading practices and validity. *Educational Measurement: Issues and Practice*, pp. 35–36.

Chappuis, J. (2005). Helping students understand assessment. *Educational Leadership, 63*(3), 39–43.

Cornelius-White, J. (2007). Learner-centered teacher-student relationships are effective: A meta-analysis. *Review of Educational Research, 77*(1), 113–143.

Cross, L. H., & R. B. Frary. (1996, April). *Hodgepodge grading: Endorsed by students and teachers alike.* Paper presented at the annual meeting of the National Council on Measurement in Education, New York, NY.

D'Andrea-O'Brien, C., & Buono, A. F. (1996). Building effective learning teams: Lessons from the field. *SAM Advanced Management Journal, 69*(4), 4–9.

Deci, E. L., Koestner, R., & Ryan, M. R. (1999). A meta-analytic review of experiments examining the effects of extrinsic rewards on intrinsic motivation. *Psychological Bulletin, 125*, 627–668.

DiPaola, M. F., & Hoy, W. K. (2014). *Improving instruction through supervision, evaluation, and professional development.* Charlotte, NC: Information Age Publishing.

Donovan, M. S., Bransford, J. D., & Pellegrino, J. W. (Eds.). (1999). *How people learn: Bridging research and practice.* Washington, DC: National Academies Press.

Earl, L., & Fullan, M. (2003). Using data in leadership for learning. *Cambridge Journal of Education, 33*(3), 383–394.

Edmondson, A. (1999). Psychological safety and learning behavior in work teams. *Administrative Science Quarterly, 44*(2), 350–383.

Edmondson, A. C. (2002). *Managing the risk of learning: Psychological safety in work teams.* Cambridge, MA: Division of Research, Harvard Business School.

Erickson, F. (2007). Some thoughts on "proximal" formative assessment of student learning. *Yearbook of the National Society for the Study of Education, 106*(1), 186–216.

Fisher, D., & Frey, N. (2007). *Checking for understanding: Formative assessment techniques for your classroom.* Alexandria, VA: Association for Supervision and Curriculum Development.

Frary, R. B., Cross, L. H., & Weber, L. J. (1993). Testing and grading practices and opinions of secondary teachers of academic subjects: Implications for instruction in measurement. *Educational Measurement: Issues and Practice, 12*(3), 23–30.

Fuchs, D., & Fuchs, L. S. (1986). Test procedure bias: A meta-analysis of examiner familiarity effects. *Review of Educational Research, 56,* 243–262.

Fullan, M. (2001). *Leading in a culture of change.* San Francisco, CA: Jossey-Bass.

Fullan, M. (2007). *The new meaning of educational change.* New York, NY: Routledge.

Gipps, C., McCallum, B., & Hargreaves, E. (2000). *What makes a good primary school teacher? Expert classroom strategies.* London, England: Routledge.

Gullickson, A. R. (1993). Matching measurement instruction to classroom-based evaluation: Perceived discrepancies, needs, and challenges. In S. L. Wise (Ed.), *Teacher training in measurement and assessment skills* (pp. 1–25). Lincoln: Buros Institute of Mental Measurement, University of Nebraska-Lincoln.

Haertel, E., & Herman, J. L. (2005). *A historical perspective on validity arguments for accountability testing.* Los Angeles, CA: National Center for Research on Evaluation, Standards, and Student Testing, Center for the Study of Evaluation, Graduate School of Education & Information.

Hall, G., & Hord, S. (2000). *Implementing change: Patterns, principles, and potholes.* Boston, MA: Allyn and Bacon.

Halverson, R., Grigg, J., Prichett, R., & Thomas, C. (2007). The new instructional leadership: Creating data-driven instructional systems in schools. *Journal of School Leadership, 17*(2), 159–194.

Hannaway, J., & Hamilton, L. (2008). *Performance-based accountability policies: Implications for school and classroom practices.* Washington, DC: Urban Institute and RAND Corporation.

Hattie, J. (1999, April). *Influences on student learning* [Inaugural lecture]. University of Auckland, New Zealand.

Hattie, J. (2003). *Teachers make a difference: What is the research evidence?* Camberwell: Australian Council for Educational Research.

Hattie, J. (2009). Visible learning: A synthesis of over 800 meta-analyses relating to achievement. London and New York, NY: Routledge.

Hattie, J. (2013). *Visible learning: A synthesis of over 800 meta-analyses relating to achievement.* London and New York, NY: Routledge.

Hattie, J., & Marsh, H. W. (1996). The relationship between research and teaching: A meta-analysis. *Review of Educational Research, 66*(4), 507–542.

Hattie, J., & Timperley, H. (2007). The power of feedback. *Review of Educational Research, 77*(1), 81–112.

Heritage, M., Lee, J., Chen, E., & LaTorre, D. (2005). *Upgrading America's use of information to improve student performance* (CSE Report 661). Los Angeles, CA: National Center for Research on Evaluation, Standards, and Student Testing.

Kegan, R., & Lahey, L. L. (2009). *Immunity to change: How to overcome it and unlock potential in yourself and your organization.* Cambridge, MA: Harvard Business Press.

Killion, J., & Bellamy, G. T. (2000). On the job. *Journal of Staff Development 21*(1), 27–31.

Langer, J. A. (2000). Excellence in English in middle and high school: How teachers' professional lives support student achievement. *American Educational Research Journal, 37*, 397–439.

Little, J.W., & Center for Action Research, I. O. (1981). *School success and staff development: The role of staff development in urban desegregated schools.* Washington, DC: National Institute of Education.

Little, J. W. (1990). "The Persistence of Privacy: Autonomy and Initiative in Teachers' Professional Relations," *Teachers College Record,* pp. 509–36.

Marzano, R. J. (2001). A new era of school reform: Going where the research takes us. Aurora, CO: Mid-continent Research for Education and Learning.

Marzano, R. J. (2003). *What works in schools: Translating research into action.* Alexandria, VA: Association for Supervision and Curriculum Development.

Marzano, R. J. (2006). *Classroom assessment & grading that work.* Alexandria, VA: Association for Supervision and Curriculum Development.

Marzano, R. J., & Mid-Continent Regional Educational Lab, A. O. (1998). *A theory-based meta-analysis of research on instruction*. Aurora, CO: Mid-continent Research for Education and Learning.

Mayer, R. E. (2002). Rote versus meaningful learning. *Theory Into Practice, 41*(4), 226–232.

McMillan, J., Myran, S., & Workman, D. (2002). Elementary teachers' classroom assessment and grading practices. *Journal of Educational Research, 95*(4), 203–213.

McMillan, J. H., & Nash, S. (2000). *Teacher classroom assessment and grading practices decision making*. Richmond, VA: Metropolitan Educational Research Consortium.

Meece, J. L., Herman, P., & McCombs, B. L. (2003). Relations of learner-centered teaching practices to adolescents' achievement goals. *International Journal of Educational Research, 39*(4), 457–475.

Mintrop, H., & Trujillo, T. (2005). *Corrective action in low-performing schools: Lessons for NCLB implementation from state and district strategies in first-generation accountability systems* (CSE Report 657). Los Angeles, CA: National Center for Research on Evaluation, Standards, and Student Testing.

Moss, C. M., & Brookhart, S. M. (2009). *Advancing formative assessment in every classroom*. Alexandria, VA: Association for Supervision and Curriculum Development.

Piaget, J. (1968). *Six psychological studies*. New York, NY: Random House.

Piaget, J. (1971). The theory of stages in cognitive development.

Pintrich, P. R. (2003). A motivational science perspective on the role of student motivation in learning and teaching contexts. *Journal of Educational Psychology, 95*(4), 667.

Plake, B. S., & Impara, J. C. (1993, April). *Teacher assessment literacy: Development of training modules*. Paper presented at the annual meeting of the National Council on Measurement in Education, Atlanta, GA.

Popham, W. J. (2006). Assessment for learning: An endangered species? *Educational Leadership, 63*(5), 82–83.

Preuss, P. (2003). *School leader's guide to root case analysis*. Larchmont, NY: Eye on Education.

Robinson, V. (2007). The impact of leadership on student outcomes: Making sense of the evidence. In *The Leadership challenge: Improving learning in schools (conference proceedings)* (pp. 12–16). Camberwell, Victoria: Australia Council for Educational Research.

Robinson, V. M., Lloyd, C. A., & Rowe, K. J. (2008). The impact of leadership on student outcomes: An analysis of the differential effects of leadership types. *Educational Administration Quarterly, 44*(5), 635–674.

Schmoker, M. (2004). Learning communities at the crossroads: Toward the best schools we've ever had. *Phi Delta Kappan, 86*(1), 84–88.

Scriven, M. (1967). The methodology of evaluation. In R.W. Tyler, R. M. Gagné & M. Scriven (Eds.), *Perspectives of curriculum evaluation* (Vol. 1, pp. 39–83). Chicago, IL: Rand McNally.

Skilton-Sylvester, P. (1999). Teaching without charisma: Involving third-graders in investigating their inner-city neighborhood. In *Making justice our project: Teachers' approaches to whole language and critical pedagogy* (pp. 115–143). New York, NY: National Council of Teachers of English.

Skilton-Sylvester, P. (2003). Less like a robot: A comparison of change in an inner-city school and a *Fortune* 500 company. *American Educational Research Journal, 40*(1), 3–41.

Spillane, J. P. (2000). Cognition and policy implementation: District policy-makers and the reform of mathematics education. *Cognition and Instruction, 18*(2), 141–179.

Spillane, J. P., Halverson, R., & Diamond, J. B. (2001, April). Investigating school leadership practice: A distributed perspective. *Educational Researcher*, pp. 23–28.

Stage, S. A., & Quiroz, D. R. (1997). A meta-analysis of interventions to decrease disruptive classroom behavior in public education settings. *School Psychology Review.*

Starratt, R. J. (2004). *Ethical leadership* (Vol. 8). Jossey-Bass.

Stiggins, R. (2005a). From formative assessment to assessment for learning: A path to success in standards-based schools. *Phi Delta Kappan, 87*(4), 324–328.

Stiggins, R. (2005b). *Student-involved classroom assessment* (4th ed.). Upper Saddle River, NJ: Pearson Merrill Prentice Hall.

Stiggins, R. (2006). Assessment for learning: A key to motivation and achievement. *Edge: The Latest Information for the Education Practitioner, 2*(2), 1–19.

Stiggins, R. (2007). Assessment through the student's eyes. *Educational Leadership, 64*(8), 22.

Stiggins, R., & Chappuis, J. (2005). Using student-involved classroom assessment to close achievement gaps. *Theory Into practice, 44*(1), 11–18.

Stiggins, R., & Conklin, N. F. (1992). *In teacher's hands: Investigating the practices of classroom assessment.* Albany, NY: SUNY Press.

Stiggins, R. L. (2002). Assessment crisis: The absence of assessment FOR learning. *Phi Delta Kappan, 83*(10), 758–765.

Thompson, M., & Wiliam, D. (2007, April). *Tight but loose: A conceptual framework for scaling up school reforms.* Paper presented at the annual meeting of the American Educational Research Association, Chicago, IL.

Thrupp, M., Mansell, H., Hawksworth, L., & Harold, B. (2003). "Schools can make a difference"—but do teachers, heads and governors really agree? *Oxford Review of Education, 29*(4), 471–484.

Tomlinson, C.A., & Moon, T. R. (2013). *Assessment and student success in a differentiated classroom.* Alexandria, VA: Association for Supervision and Curriculum Development.

Tschannen-Moran, M., Woolfolk Hoy, A., & Hoy, W. K. (1998). Teacher efficacy: Its meaning and measure. *Review of Educational Research, 68*(2), 202–248.

Vander Ark, T. (2002). The case for small high schools. *Educational Leadership, 59*(5), 55–59.

Vosniadou, S. (2001). *How children learn* (Educational Practices Series—7). Geneva Switzerland: International Bureau of Education; Brussels, Belgium: International Academy of Education.

Vosniadou, S. (2003). How children learn. In *Successful Schooling* (pp. 16–33). New Delhi, India: Discover Publishing Houses.

Wade, H.H. (2001). *Data inquiry and analysis for educational reform.* Eugene, OR: ERIC Clearinghouse on Educational Management. Retrieved from ERIC database. (ED461911)

Wayman, J. C., Cho, V., & Johnston, M. T. (2007). *The data-informed district: A district-wide evaluation of data use in the Natrona County School District.* Austin: The University of Texas.

Wayman, J. C., Midgley, S., & Stringfield, S. (2006). Leadership for data-based decision-making: Collaborative data teams. In A. Danzig, K. Borman, B. Jones, & B. Wright (Eds.), *New models of professional development for learner centered leadership* (pp. 189–206). Mahwah, NJ: Erlbaum.

Weinberger, E., & McCombs, B. L. (2001, April). *The impact of learner-centered practices on the academic and non-academic outcomes of upper elementary and middle school students.* Paper presented at the annual meeting of the American Educational Research Association, Seattle, WA.

Welsh, M., Eastwood, M., & D'Agostino, J. (2014). Conceptualizing teaching to the test under standards-based reform. *Applied Measurement in Education.* Retrieved from www.tandfonline.com/doi/abs/10.1080/08957347.2014.880439

Wergin, J. (2003). Departments that work: Building and sustaining cultures of excellence in academic programs. Williston, VT: *Anker Publishing Company, Inc.*

West, M., & Anderson, M. (1996). Innovations in top management teams. *Journal of Applied Psychology, 31*(6), 680–693.

West, M. A. (2000). Reflexivity, revolution, and innovation in work teams. In M. M. Beyerlein, D. A. Johnson, & S. T. Beyerlein (Eds.), *Advances in interdisciplinary studies of work teams* (Vol. 5, pp. 1–29). Greenwich, CT: JAI Press.

Wiburg, K., & Brown, S. (2007). *Lesson study communities.* Thousand Oaks, CA: Corwin.

Wiggins, G., & McTighe, J. (1998). *Understanding by design.* Alexandria, VA: Association for Supervision and Curriculum Development.

Index

Note: Page numbers in *italics* indicate figures or tables.